D0848854

Advisory Editor

KENNETH E. CARPENTER
Curator, Kress Library
Graduate School of Business Administration
Harvard University

DEMANDS
FOR EARLY CLOSING HOURS

Three Pamphlets

1843

Arno Press

A New York Times Company/New York 1972

397378

Reprint Edition 1972 by Arno Press Inc.

Reprinted from copies in the Kress Library
Graduate School of Business Administration,
Harvard University

BRITISH LABOUR STRUGGLES: CONTEMPORARY PAMPHLETS 1727-1850
ISBN for complete set: 0-405-04410-0

See last pages for complete listing.

Manufactured in the United States of America

Library of Congress Cataloging in Publication Data
Main entry under title:

Demands for early closing hours.

     (British labour struggles:
contemporary pamphlets 1727-1850)
     Reprint of A word for early closing, by T. Honiborne,
first published about 1843; The wrongs of our youth, by
R. B. Grindrod, first published 1843; and of Prize essay
on the evils which are produced by later hours of
business, by T. Davies, first published 1843.
     1. Hours of labor--Great Britain.   I.   Honiborne,
Thomas.   A word for early closing.   II.   Grindrod, Ralph
Barnes, 1811-1883.   The wrongs of our youth.
III.   Davies, Thomas.   Prize essay on the evils which
are produced by late hours of business.
IV.   Series.
HD5166.D45   331.2'572   72-2523
ISBN 0-405-04416-X

Harriet Irving Library

NOV 7 1972

University of New Brunswick

Contents

Honiborne, Thomas
A word for early closing: embracing a view of the evils connected with the late hour system of business; and showing the advantages resulting from an abridgment of the same, to the employer, the employed, and the public . . . London, D. Bicknell [etc., 1843?]

Grindrod, Ralph Barnes
The wrongs of our youth: an essay on the evils of the late-hour system . . . London, W. Brittain, and G. Gilpin [etc., etc.] 1843.

Davies, Thomas
Prize essay on the evils which are produced by late hours of business, and on the benefits which would attend their abridgement . . . With a preface by the Hon. and Rev. Baptist W. Noel . . . London, J. Nisbet and co., 1843.

A

WORD FOR EARLY CLOSING:

EMBRACING A VIEW OF THE EVILS

CONNECTED WITH

THE LATE HOUR SYSTEM OF BUSINESS;

AND SHOWING THE ADVANTAGES RESULTING FROM

AN ABRIDGMENT OF THE SAME,

TO THE

EMPLOYER, THE EMPLOYED, AND THE PUBLIC.

BY THOMAS HONIBORNE.

"At bona pars hominum decepta cupidine falso,
Nil satis est, inquit ; quia tanti, quantum habeas, sis.
Quid facias illi ? jubeas miserum esse libenter
Quatenus id facit."

LONDON:

DAVID BICKNELL, COLEMAN STREET;
T. ARNOLD, PATERNOSTER ROW.

PRICE SIXPENCE.

J. Rider, Printer, 14, Bartholomew Close, London.

A WORD FOR EARLY CLOSING.

COMMERCE, more or less, has been engaged in by mankind, in almost all ages and countries. Although it cannot be precisely ascertained at what period it commenced, yet there is evidence that it existed at a very remote age. The manner in which it was transacted, was by exchanging commodities then in use, for others. Gradually it assumed a new aspect amongst the ancient nations; first in navigation on inland rivers, and then in men traversing seas separating one country from another, and conveying the productions of other lands to their own. It was carried to a great extent by the Egyptians, Tyrians, and their colony the Carthaginians. Upon the destruction of these states, it continued to flourish under the governments of Greece and Rome. And although it suffered a great decline by the destruction of the Roman empire, yet it was not annihilated, but existed in some of the states in Italy.

In more modern times, commerce was engaged in by most of the European nations, which acquired, through it, both wealth and power. By degrees, England, though never insensible to its importance, yet excited by the successful exertions of her continental neighbours, became in it much superior to them. As her trade became extended, her importance and power increased; and, at the present time, most commercial nations are more or less tributary to British industry.

Many advantages accrue to a country from its commerce. Its national character is derived from its principal engagements, which, when commercial, place it in an important situation. The feelings and habits of each inhabitant are, in some measure, formed and strengthened by his occupation. When engaged in traffic, it frequently becomes superior to other nations. The industry of its inhabitants is excited, their invention called into action, and their local prejudices removed from them. By these means, wealth is acquired, enabling it to provide resources, beyond the reach of others, in the extremity of danger, and frequently to maintain a firm resistance against attempts made to oppress its inhabitants. Cities comparatively small, have sometimes been thus able to continue a hazardous struggle, for a long period, against the most powerful monarch existing, so as to frustrate his exertions, and excite his rage. Engagements in traffic have also great influence in forming the character of those. engaged in it. They are not distinguished by those contracted habits which others of different occupation acquire from it. Their attention is constantly fixed upon some topic connected with trade, or other subjects of importance. Those who are eminent in mercantile affairs, are also men of activity and decision of character, acquired frequently by engagements in them. They obtain an insight into human character with greater facility than other men.

These advantages, however, connected with those whose engagements are commercial, are not unalloyed with evils arising from the same source. They are such as are deeply to be deplored, and require the cause of them to be removed with all expedition. The nature of man, ever grasping and avaricious, has seized every opportunity presented to acquire wealth. And, not considering that from ten to twelve hours daily are sufficient for all secular engagements, it has devoted to them time which the claims of God and nature require should be given to improvement of the mind and body. Although a sufficiency for all the purposes of life might be, and often is, acquired in a much shorter space of time, yet every moment in which a trifling sum can be obtained, has been seized upon, and devoted to the pursuits of trade, to the great injury of the intellectual, physical, and moral condition of those employed in it. Men, in whom selfishness was predominant, notwithstanding their excellent qualities, have carried the late hour system of business to a length which leaves no time for engagements of a higher and nobler nature. This system, adopted by our ancestors, has been transmitted to their posterity, and become so universal, that now mercantile men, willing to abridge the time devoted to business, are compelled to maintain it from the conviction that, unless they do, their trade will decline, and their competitors reap the advantage.

When business is engaged in so long daily, it becomes irksome to the parties employed, and renders them unfit for other things. The mind of man cannot be exercised incessantly upon a single subject, without becoming incompetent either for suitable attention to it, or to any other object of pursuit. It is unfitted even for subjects which would create hilarity at any other time, and might be indulged in with profit. If the attention were directed and fixed upon any matter requiring strong thought for a few hours, the mind could then be unbent by other engagements. It might be diverted by things of a more interesting nature, by which it would be relieved from intense thought, and prepared to engage with profit on the same subject, or on others requiring an equal degree of attention. The interval might be employed in obtaining important information—gaining an insight into human nature—or qualifying the frame for the more suitable discharge of duty. Affairs occurring daily in life, examined with attention, would yield, at once, interest and profit. This not being done, two evils arise:

a gradual dislike to business, and slow improvement in other things. It is often the case, that the mind, employed unremittingly upon any matter for a long period, contracts a dislike to it, though when first the attention was directed to it, delight was experienced. Extreme thought upon it renders it unattractive. This is seen in business with respect to some of the employed. There is required from them continual exércise of reflection, either as to the best manner in which they can effect most sales, or sometimes even concerning what ought to be executed at the time. When there happens to be a press of business, much attention and mental reasoning are employed, to despatch it with the least possible delay. Forethought is necessary in the process, so as to execute it with the least inconvenience. When every thing is prepared, extreme attention is required in completing it. In addition to these, there are sometimes other duties requiring still the same degree of attention, but which it is impossible to accomplish in a reasonable time. Hence, on these occasions, it is no uncommon thing for the parties to be employed in them beyond midnight, to the great injury of their bodies and minds. Cases have occurred in which are seen the disastrous effects of this practice. The health has been destroyed; the mental faculties temporarily impaired, and consequently no employment. And at other times, even when there is nothing absolutely necessary to be done, there is a necessity to exercise the invention for some employment. For these reasons, business, which ought to yield pleasure, becomes irksome.

Another evil, in many establishments, is its depriving them of the power to avail themselves of the means of improvement. Moderate engagements in business would be beneficial, tending to produce a habit of restraining feelings, better suppressed—inuring the mind to attention, and to take a circumstantial view of affairs; but when they exceed a certain limit, they become injurious, making the mind wearied, and incapable of engaging with profit in other pursuits.

An intelligent young man, in any trade where late hours are kept, really anxious to improve himself, when business is over, by literary pursuits, is unable to attain his object. If he is desirous of reading some interesting portion of history, he cannot gain advantage from his attempt to read; for his mind, jaded by the labour of the day, is unable to keep up its attention even for a short period. It is the same with respect to other subjects which, to some, might be more interesting. In science, in Christian morality, the same effects are produced from the same cause, and not from any want of desire to gain information, or strengthen the moral sense.

Since no pleasure is derived from reading, it is sought for elsewhere. The feelings having been under restraint the whole day, whenever an opportunity presents itself for indulging them, are engaged on objects tending to lead them away from what is serious, to trifling and levity. The manner in which many of the employed in all trades pass their time after the hours of business, depraves the intellectual taste, and creates a relish for unworthy objects. It is often the case, that the natural inclination becomes apparently changed, by the attention being daily employed upon no other topics than those connected with frivolity. Although many, on their first introduction to these circles, are not much disposed to indulge in it, yet gradually their reserve is removed, so that some of them become distinguished by their superior manner of introducing and supporting it. This, however, is only a prelude to more fearful consequences. As an illustration of these remarks, a case which frequently occurs may be introduced, of a youth entering some house of business, where the morals of the employed are but little regarded, becoming contaminated by bad example, and eventually almost ruined. He is sent by his parents, in the fond hope of becoming an excellent character. He enters the establishment, and at first is fearful of engaging in the pursuits which he sees before him; but, day after day rolling on, they become familiar to him, nor does he view them with that apprehension which he at first entertained with respect to them. Nor does the bad influence rest here; if so, the evil resulting would be comparatively trifling. He gradually practises what he at first shunned beholding. His mind has become so perverted by bad example, not counteracted by reasoning and reflection, for which he has neither time nor inclination that, from levity, he proceeds to immorality. He contracts bad habits, which give rise to other evils of a more distressing nature; soon mingles in society still more corrupt, by the influence of which he becomes more depraved, and is reduced to an almost incurable condition.

Though much of this is traceable to the morals not being cultivated with proper care in the establishment which the youth enters, yet it also arises, partially, from being confined so long to one engagement. The nature of man requires variety, in order to employ all its faculties; and when some, whether of body or mind, are not exercised sufficiently, and others too much, an uneasy sensation is experienced, which seeks relief frequently in some improper object. The necessary variety cannot be obtained, because of the lengthened time devoted to business. A continual sameness is therefore felt, and amusement not being derived from profitable engagements, is sought for in things approaching to immorality.

This general view, however, will convey but an imperfect idea of the evils connected with late hour trading. They affect the intellectual, physical, and moral condition of the employed. Many of them being intelligent, and desirous of information, have been accommodated, in some of the larger establishments, with libraries provided by the employers. Wishing to improve their minds by knowledge, they are anxious to engage in such reading as shall be beneficial to them. Their wish, however, is frequently frustrated from want of time to profit by this circumstance. If time were afforded them, there is no question that much of it would be spent in perusing the literary works of the age. Some benefit is derived from them, but not so much as is desirable, and which might be obtained if the hours of business were shorter; for it is not possible that they whose minds have been employed during the day on different subjects, should suddenly transfer an equal degree of attention to others. It will be surprising to many, that so much literary information should be acquired by them, considering how much time is devoted by them to business.

Such desultory information, however, is below the station of society in which they stand. They ought to be possessed of knowledge far more extensive; for it is not the case in the present day, as it was several centuries back, that only a few possess information at all worth the knowing; but it has become generally diffused, to a degree not known in the previous history of the country. Whilst the literary men of the land stand high in their professions, there are others, making no pretensions to the literary character, who are by no means deficient in information, as well on subjects not connected with their peculiar engagements, as in them. The means of acquiring knowledge are so numerous and so accessible to all, that it is morally impossible for many not to make a great advancement in it. Much important information is now collected by the industry of the existing generation, concerning subjects which, a few years ago, could be known only to those trained in the pursuits of learning. It is on this account that many whose rank in society is inferior, are often better informed than those above them. Their opportunities for improvement are more numerous than those enjoyed by most persons in business of any description, since the time is comparatively brief which they devote to their ordinary employments. These have not been lost sight of, nor misimproved, by the intelligent amongst them, who have become, by this means, in respect of knowledge on general subjects, superior to many others, whose station in life would be filled with more credit, if they were better acquainted with different transactions and events. Facts like these evidently display great improvement in the intellectual condition of some of our countrymen, and at the same time furnish a strong argument for the abridgment of the time devoted to business. For, in the neglect of this, the class of persons alluded to, will take precedence of those above them: there will be a reversion in the state of society, on account of the accumulated knowledge of the one, and the lack of information in the other;—an effect which will be produced by the late hour trading, if persevered in, and not from any want of exertion used by those employed in business, to improve themselves; for knowledge, which makes a man superior in many respects to others destitute of it, is only to be acquired by that application which they are unable to give to it. Many improvements in various branches of art have been introduced by means of extended information; and if knowledge be progressive, more will be effected, rendering the names of the inventors celebrated, and the class of persons to which they belong, more important in society. Then it will become absolutely impossible for those engaged in business, to keep pace with the improved state of society, unless they devote more time to objects which strengthen the intellectual faculties.

The evil, however, does not rest here, but will be more clearly seen in future life. Then, many will occupy the place of employers, and in this capacity exercise a powerful influence, either for good or evil, over those associated or in any way connected with them. If they become eminent as mercantile men, and are at the same time destitute of general information which others have acquired, they will be unqualified to fill such stations as they might occupy with advantage, provided there were combined in their character both the qualifications of a merchant, and information upon general topics. Upon this supposition, they would exercise a very beneficial influence over society, and by their exertions could perform much good to their fellow-creatures. Their information on former transactions, conjoined with their knowledge of business, would qualify them for engaging in any matter of importance, with greater advantage to themselves and others. If, however, they continue in their present condition with but slight information, their influence will not be so beneficial when they are placed in different stations in society. Although they may have every requisite to conduct their own affairs with precision, yet they will be unable to engage in occasional transactions of importance, without frequently doing injury both to themselves and others. There will be required in many engagements (not indeed connected with their peculiar business, but which it will be sometimes expedient for them to be employed in) much general knowledge to transact affairs with exactness. The information requisite will be such as can be acquired more expeditiously, if not only, by daily attention upon recorded matters of fact; and a man ignorant of them will be rendered unqualified for such engagements. When he is employed in them without possessing the prerequisites, it is manifest that much error will be exhibited, both to his own discredit and the disadvantage of others.

Again, the character of a nation may be frequently learned from its literary productions. They show not merely its most talented minds, but likewise the kind of knowledge which is generally sought after. If information be much diffused, there will be a greater demand for works of excellence; for in proportion as a community becomes well-informed, it is able to distinguish between works of merit and those which are worthless. It will discover with a glance, and receive immediately, what is excellent. This will constitute the standard literature of the country. It will suggest to a foreigner, with tolerable accuracy, ideas respecting the nation to which the writer belongs. It will afford also to others copious matter for reasoning upon the character of their own countrymen. These advantages ought not, however, to be exclusive to such persons. The literary man and the man of business should alike enjoy them, both for profit and information.

But such information cannot be well acquired by those employed so long in business, from not having time to give suitable attention to it. Hence they will often, from necessity, be ignorant of much important knowledge.

The evils connected with the late hour system of business affect the employed also physically. It is necessary that they should be unremitting in their attention to business, as their engagements are of such a nature as to require it. Confinement to it from thirteen to fourteen hours daily, with but few opportunities to use the best means of recruiting their strength, acts injuriously upon them. The whole day, except a small portion of time, is taken up in the engagements of trade. The moment almost after rising, something connected with it must be done, as in making preparation for the engagements of the day, which, though unremittingly attended to, yet are frequently not finished, when apparently nothing else is required. Many are often occupied after this time, in disposing into order what has been laid by quickly and without arrangement. Nor are there opportunities for counteracting the ill effects produced by these practices. They cannot seize them even in those seasons of the day set apart for taking refreshment; the time allotted being so exceedingly brief. The claims of business are still urgent at that time. If there were but moderate time in the day allowed for this purpose, a portion of it at least might be spent in recruiting the strength for the remaining engagements. This, however, cannot be done, either at this time or at any other, except in some few establishments. In general, there are but few opportunities for it; and a man cannot be continually laying himself under obligation to his employer, by requesting permission for this object, when others are compelled to remain in trade. It is only occasionally that it is obtained, but at such long intervals that the injury sustained by close attention and long confinement cannot be repaired by recreation at that time. There are indeed occasions when some leave for business purposes; but they do not occur so frequently as to require more than a few to be absent, and that a comparatively short time. The larger number are retained within, unable to enjoy the privilege of leaving the establishment. Confinement so long, and attention so severe, have a very injurious effect, producing a morbid state of feeling. This is constantly experienced by those whose occupations deprive them of out-door exercise. Nothing induces this sooner than long confinement. The words of an eminent physician, applied, however, to another branch of employment, may be used appropriately with respect to them: "The almost total privation of exercise, the late hours, and the long duration of their work, are more than sufficient to injure, if not destroy, their health in a few years."* It will be found, accordingly, that many suffer from physical causes, not at first to so great a degree as to require them to leave their employment; but they are

---

* Dr. Clark on Consumption and Scrofula, page 201.

affected by a gradual diminution of that robust health which they enjoyed when commencing their occupation. It is a fact not to be controverted, that many become eventually, from too close confinement to business, in a state needing the advice and aid of the physician, and that, after frequent application, they are but little improved, as they are unable to attend to his directions respecting their taking more exercise. Neglecting this they bring upon themselves the evils which they endure.

Were the majority of them uneducated, it is probable that still greater injury would be experienced; but many of them, in consequence of education, aware of the injury likely to result from their employment, avoid it partially by the regulation of the mind, and the cultivation of morality. If persons of an inferior grade in society were placed in the same situation which they hold, the bad effects would be more speedily apparent; for, being accustomed to different habits, they could not sustain the fatigue consequent from their new employment. There are other reasons also which prevent the bad effects becoming more generally known. Whenever some of them suffer so much as to be necessitated to leave their occupation, the places which they filled are taken by others, and they are frequently forgotten amidst various engagements. They retire to their own homes, where they use the best means prescribed for recruiting health, or enter some other employment more conducive to their comfort and safety. Those, again, in whom the bad effects have taken such hold as to be immoveable, pine away in some locality distant from the scene of their employments, where their occupation is entirely forgotten or unknown.

Nor is there any way of removing these evils, except by adopting the system of early closing. Many, though conscious that they are injuring both body and mind, and though desirous of benefiting themselves, yet cannot often accomplish their wish; the places where late traffic is not practised being so few, that it becomes a great difficulty to procure employment in them. Hence there is no other alternative for many of them, but to continue in their employment, with the probable loss of health, but with emolument for their exertions; or to throw themselves upon society, with more opportunities for preserving it, but with no further gain accruing to them.

As there is not sufficient time for improving the intellectual and physical faculties, so it is likewise with respect to their moral condition. As they cannot cultivate, to a great degree, the mind by reading, so they cannot sufficiently improve the moral affections of their nature. The most suitable means of promoting this is by being under the influence of Christian morality; but it cannot be exercised so strongly and extensively as is fit, from the slender knowledge possessed of it, arising from the short space of time in which they can peruse the directions of Holy Writ. Some would be induced to study them more, if they enjoyed more opportunities. Too little time also is appropriated to the claims of Christian morality upon the service and homage of man to the Creator; which would be rendered with greater profit to the worshipper, were not his mind so much fatigued, and his feelings so much weakened, by the arduous labours of the day. These operate with injurious effect upon some, who, if time were allowed, would engage in these acts with advantage to themselves, but now neglect them. The influence, therefore, of these exercises not being sufficiently felt, many are deprived of much benefit always resulting from them.

There are other evils also arising from this system. As many are unable to take recreation on any other day than Sunday, they avail themselves of the opportunities then offered for this purpose. Although some may strongly contend that there is no moral evil in this, since it is rendered expedient by long confinement during the week, yet they could not but allow, when observing the evils exhibited on this day more than on any other, that those who act thus are likely to contract habits of a pernicious tendency. Even upon the supposition that the arguments were sufficiently strong to justify the practice, still there are so many evils connected with it as to require its abandonment. There is more immorality practised and witnessed on that day than on any other. It is augmented by the numerous facilities which are then afforded for indulging it. And it is almost impossible for any individual who engages in such recreation on that day as is commonly adopted, however morally disposed he may be, to escape the attendant evils. The vast number who spend the day in this manner is almost incredible. A year or two ago the number of those from all parts of the metropolis who went short excursions to various places on that day, exceeded the number of the whole population of London within the walls.* Most of them do not consider it pleasure, unless they obtain whatever might minister to their gratification. These practices have a very injurious effect, not only on those who engage in them, but upon others disinclined to them, by influencing them to consider too lightly of such habits, and eventually to fall into them. If, then, recreation, when taken on a Sunday, is productive of such evils, it cannot be justified by any arguments. Although, however, the conduct of those acting thus, cannot be cleared from censure by the plea that it arises from their not being able to take recreation at another time, it does not follow that this has no influence in exciting to the practice. On the contrary, late hour trading is often the occasion of it; and were another system adopted, it would not be engaged in by so many, at least there could not be then any plausible reason to urge for it.

When there is neither time nor opportunity for moral improvement, much carelessness will prevail respecting every subject in connexion with it. Thought concerning Christian morality being but seldom cherished, it will not exercise such beneficial influence as it might; and the longer the interval in which no reflection upon

* City Mission Magazine, January, 1843.

it is made, of the less importance it will be considered, becoming eventually entirely disregarded. The reception which it generally meets with amongst men who consider it a matter of no consequence whether it be regarded at all, will contribute much to this. From constant association with men of this character, many become quite indifferent to it. Hence much immorality exists amongst those who entertain these notions, produced by not enjoying opportunities for moral improvement. Habits are contracted which, unless counteracted by some other influence, would be productive of much injury. It is well that the extent to which they lead is not fully seen, from the hazard of losing connexion with the establishment in which it should be exhibited.

Those who are moral, but not actually religious, are affected by the late hour system of business. As they are constantly engaged in exertions to acquire wealth, whether it be gained or not, they gradually form notions respecting it inconsistent with truth. In consequence of a continual pursuit of it, they are induced to consider it as the chief good. Being made of so much importance by almost all with whom they associate, and the time devoted to its acquisition being so long, a notion is formed in the mind which it is difficult to remove. Many, entering houses of business early in life, and seeing the importance attached to it, are, as it were, trained up in an idea that nothing else is worthy of being compared to it. When they perceive it pursued with so much eagerness, to the neglect of other things which, probably, they were early taught to consider more momentous, they gradually infer that the notions instilled into their minds then were incorrect, and learn to regard wealth alone as worthy of their most strenuous endeavours and perseverance. Such sentiments as these are, in many, extremely prejudicial to the growth of moral affections to which they are naturally inclined. The means by which they are acquired, apart from Christian motives, is in cultivating the mind by reading and reflection, so as to form it to a taste for things noble and virtuous. By this would be seen the very little share which wealth alone has in promoting human happiness; and that only when possessed in combination with purity of motive, exalted notions of virtue, and the practice of virtuous actions, it becomes a blessing; without which it will never yield permanent satisfaction. The very little time enjoyed for acquiring such notions, induces false ideas of its value, and urges men to pursue it with too great avidity, to the neglect, frequently, of duty to God, their neighbour, and themselves.

In order to notice all who sustain injury, it should be remembered, that there are some amongst the employed, indifferent to the claims of morality, who, if their own interest could be promoted, would not hesitate to act dishonourably. It is not meant that there are more of this character here than elsewhere. They are to be found in every class of society, whether devoted to business or other pursuits. Every one knows the influence which example has over others. It is more efficacious frequently than instruction. A good example will often be productive of the greatest blessings. It spreads its beneficial influence secretly, though surely, amongst others, and often engages them to imitate it. If, therefore, it were placed before the indifferent, by the moral and the religious, it would in all probability cause them at the least to reflect upon the worth of morality, if not eventually to embrace it. Were he to see men more constantly actuated entirely by motives of virtue, seldom, if ever, deviating from the path of rectitude, what a beneficial influence might be exercised over him! This, however, he cannot have, because of all being constantly engaged in trade. If there were a curtailment of the time, the example would then be exhibited. The moral, employing their opportunities in the cultivation of the mind, and the religious, attending to engagements congenial to their tastes, would afford an example of excellence worthy of imitation.

From these considerations, then, it appears that the religious, the moral, and those indifferent to morality, experience much evil from the late hour system of business. But it will be objected by some, that, provided the time appropriated to trade were abridged, the condition of the employed would be even worse than it is now, since they would have better opportunities for following the bad tendency of their own minds. It is of great benefit, it is said, to have no facility whatever to indulge this propensity. There are some who, if permitted to venture out in the evening, would contract many bad habits, and injure themselves to a degree incurable; and there would be great danger of their falling into practices bringing disgrace both upon themselves and the establishments with which they might be connected. But it should not be forgotten, that if there be a tendency in any to immoral actions, it is much strengthened by being confined too long to business, which makes them still more desirous to follow it, under whatever restraint they are placed. If the time in the evening were at their own disposal it would be weakened, and bad habits would be less easily contracted. As long confinement, by repressing the feelings, excites to their indulgence when unrestrained, so when they are not repressed too much, they will not be gratified in so great a degree when entirely free. The adoption, therefore, of early closing would be beneficial rather than injurious.

Facts, however, will shew still more the fallacy of the objection. In what manner do the majority of those pass their vacant time who leave early establishments of other kinds? Is there more immorality amongst them, or is there not rather the contrary, on that very account? Do not the larger proportion improve their time with their families, or in some other way? There is no reason whatever for presuming one class to be different from another in feelings and desires. If they improve the opportunities which they enjoy to beneficial ends, others also would do the same. These, therefore, would act in a similar manner. Sometimes acquaintances would be visited for friendly intercourse; at other times institutions would be attended for the sake of improvement; some would employ their time in pursuits congenial to their tastes; others would take recreation for the benefit of their physical condition. There is, therefore, good reason to affirm, that none of the consequences comprised in the objection, would follow, and that only those whose will is so strong that no restraint could hinder its indulgence, would act in this manner.

Having shewn the evils flowing from the system of late traffic, it will be necessary to advert to the advantages likely to result from an abridgment. It is apparent, from the considerations adduced, that the system needs alteration, by curtailing the time. As to the precise time, there can be no hesitation in saying that the maximum should be twelve hours, and the minimum eight hours, or even fewer, daily. If every establishment were closed at an early hour, there would be time afforded for the pursuits of literature, science, and morality; and the benefits resulting from it would be experienced by all parties. If this system were adopted, the employers would be relieved from anxious thoughts concerning trade, which they cannot dismiss from themselves when leaving before the hours of closure. There would be less loss sustained in the expenditure incurred by lighting. At many places it can be of no further service than to exhibit articles which are not sold at that time; and at others, in which by this means more sales are effected, by attracting some to purchase what they probably would not have thought of: the profit accruing will not often clear the expense. If early closing were adopted, there would be no loss in pecuniary matters. Upon the supposition that the same amount of business were not done then as is executed now, the loss sustained by it would be less than the expense now incurred by lighting. Although so many might not be attracted by the exhibition of merchandises in the evening, to purchase some of them, yet they would continue to provide necessary things. These, exceeding supposed superfluities purchased in consequence of the display of them, would make the amount of business done, when all closed early, nearly equal to what it is now, with the expense of lighting considerably reduced.

If, however, there were some loss sustained, there would be time acquired, which could be employed to profitable uses, making ample compensation for it. This would be an advantage to those whose attention is much engaged upon political subjects. They could reflect and reason upon different transactions, and discuss them with freedom, undisturbed by apprehension, which now they cannot but entertain, that, by engaging so much in them, they are neglecting things of more importance. If they are eminent in this department, they have devoted much time to acquire a knowledge of different circumstances and events; and it is necessary for them to do the same now to sustain their reputation. But a mercantile man attempting this, experiences greater inconveniences than others. He is frequently disturbed by the claims of business; his mind is often perplexed by reflection upon matters foreign to his purpose; it is with difficulty he can call home his thoughts, in consequence of interruption, which sometimes makes it necessary for him to retrace the steps of his reasoning. These are evils which might be remedied by early closing. Although the time which he devotes to these pursuits is as long as it would be (if not longer) provided the hours of business were curtailed, yet he cannot accomplish so much in the one case as he might in the other. If this were carried into effect, he would gain a twofold advantage: he could not only devote more time to the engagements of trade, and in all probability increase it, but he could also gain more information in a much shorter period, by being able to fix his attention entirely to the subject before him. Attending more unremittingly to business during the day, political subjects would afford pleasure when it was over, and be more expeditiously comprehended. He could then obtain more extensive knowledge of facts and events which have transpired, either ages ago amongst nations then existing, or in modern times; and of the influence which they had in forming habits or promoting civilization. When thus armed with these qualifications—extensive knowledge and great influence as a mercantile man, he could effect much good to many.

He would possess also more suitable opportunities of being acquainted with the various nations of the earth; their productions, the extent of their commerce, the true state of trade, the causes which have led to its decline or prosperity, the best means of promoting it; and of taking an enlarged view of transactions, whether domestic or foreign, their origin, progress, circumstances, and design. The greater information any person has on these and other topics, the better qualified is he to remove prejudice from himself, and, by wise conduct, from others; to advance his own prosperity, and to engage in undertakings for the benefit of others. He could not raise the common plea that, by doing so, he should be acting unjustly to himself and family, and allowing his affairs gradually to decay. All his influence could then be used towards promoting plans, having for their end the amelioration of the human race. His exertions, when attended with success, would conduce to his own advantage. The benefits communicated would be reflected back upon himself. As the light reflected from any object makes it more conspicuous, so they would render him more respected and beloved.

The abridgment of the hours devoted to business would be productive of great advantage to the employed, as well as the employers. According to the present system, it is necessary for all to be constantly occupied in something, whether it be really useful or not. An equal amount of trade is not always transacted, so as to keep every one usefully engaged in it. But when there is a press of business, much is required to be accomplished by a certain time; and also when there is slackness of it, there is still a necessity of being engaged in something frequently of no use, but yet attended with labour. At such seasons much is done merely for the sake of employment. Thus there is no equivalent for great exertions when business presses, inasmuch as active service is always demanded. The time spent in this manner is evidently lost. Also, even on days when tolerable trade is executed, so that neither party has any reason to complain—the employer, from its not clearing his expenses, and the employed, from too much being required of them—there are numerous intervals in which nothing is done of any real value. If they were collected together, and the aggregate known, they would make a large amount of time spent in nothing profitable to either party, but on the contrary really wasted. It appears, then, that the employed have much vacant time, which they could, but are unable, to improve. It is plain also that these intervals might be made much fewer, if not altogether removed, if business were finished at a reasonable time. If all agreed to an abridgment of the hours, the public would be compelled to purchase what they required at much shorter intervals; business throughout the day would be more brisk; and time enjoyed for profitable purposes.

The time thus obtained could be improved in such a manner that the employed might derive advantage from it in their intellectual, physical, and moral condition. By the cultivation of the mind, they would gain numerous and important benefits. Every man, so far as his station in life will permit, is bound to improve his reasoning faculties by the most suitable methods. Whenever, in consequence of other engagements, they cannot be cultivated to such an extent as is desirable, still they ought not to be wholly neglected; for nature has not conferred upon mankind faculties to no purpose. The various senses of the body have their proper design. If none of them were used, men would be subject to unavoidable accidents and dangers. Life would become a burden, from its numerous troubles and miseries. As the bodily faculties were given for use, so were those of the mind. In the neglect of them, errors are maintained, and prejudices cherished. Numerous mistakes are also seen in the conduct of men from the same reason. If a larger proportion of them cultivated their mental faculties with greater ardour and perseverance, so many unfavourable occurrences would not be heard of.

If they had more extensive information of facts in the history of nations and individuals, rash enterprizes would not be so frequently undertaken, bringing disgrace upon those who planned them, and misery upon others. Hence it follows, that much attention ought to be given to improve these gifts of nature; and when too small a portion of time is devoted to it, all legitimate attempts should be employed to obtain more, by bestowing less upon other engagements of minor importance. When this object is attained, advantages would be procured of great importance, amply repaying efforts, however laborious, that might be used to accomplish it.

Those desirous of intellectual improvement, having then time, would devote it to the attainment of this end, and would speedily experience the good effects of the practice. A vast amount of literary information might be acquired by employing stated seasons daily in its acquisition. If the time be comparatively short, still it would be sufficient. The mind being in a state fit for the occupation, could accomplish much. A gradual advancement would be made in knowledge important to the purposes of human life. It would be connected likewise with a degree of enjoyment. Although there is apparent equality between individuals of the same rank in society, yet he who has cultivated his mind is superior in many respects. A consciousness of its improved condition yields to him satisfaction, independent of other pleasures which he receives from it. In reading or hearing different events, greater delight is experienced in being acquainted with the circumstances connected with or leading to them. Information so extensive could not be gained by only occasionally devoting time and attention to its acquisition. It is necessary that more stated seasons should be given to it. In the progress of improvement, the mind would be strengthened, former errors removed, and knowledge increased. It is by cultivation that the mind of one man can grasp many different subjects with ability; whilst another, of equal native capacity, cannot comprehend the elements of them. The difference between two persons, of whom one has improved his mind, and the other has not, is striking. In the one case, instances of fortitude to sustain trial are met with; skill in devising plans, and wisdom and judgment in their execution. In the other, there is ignorance of many common occurrences; mistakes in conduct; no desire for more information than is absolutely necessary for existence. Such a man, by exercising no forethought, cannot anticipate the most likely events; exerts not a proper control over his feelings and passions; and cannot sustain unexpected calamities.

Advantage would be gained by occupying the attention upon human affairs, and judging accurately respecting them. There will be the acting more prudently in the transactions of life. There will be the restraining of feelings which one man might have been provoked to entertain towards another. In reflecting upon facts which have been recorded, will be seen the ill-judged actions of men in the overthrow of states, and the devastation of countries without just reason; for it is but seldom that they are the result of necessity. These affairs will be perused not as mere matters of history, necessary to be known in order to maintain with honour a certain station in society, but for the sake of being better qualified for mingling with profit amongst men, by knowing more of their actions. Unless this be an end of the occupation, the time spent in it might be better employed in other engagements. But when perused with this design, they will influence to the restraint of feelings which might otherwise be manifested. This can be, and often is, acquired by men with but little information; but it may be gained much earlier in life, and established upon a surer foundation, by taking a comprehensive view of the actions of men in all ages.

B

Another prevalent mistake of human nature might be rectified by cultivating the mind. It is considered that happiness is attainable in becoming eminent amongst men in some department for which there is a supposed adaptation. It is imagined that, in attaining to the rank of men who stand high in it, nothing more is required to render happiness complete on earth. The honour and respect which they receive, their names celebrated and sometimes transmitted to posterity, place around them a false splendour, deceiving the unwary. The means of attaining such rank in some department are perhaps accessible. Every opportunity is seized to use them, and the object is ultimately reached; but frequently by the mind being constantly engaged, and almost every moment spent, in its pursuit. Not unfrequently the justice or injustice of the means has been disregarded, the sole object being the attainment of the end. Many have the power, and can use the means, of acquiring distinction in some class in human life. The danger is that they may be tempted to conceive too highly, and to paint in too glowing colours, the object of their wishes, and having done so to use any means in its acquisition. The remedy for this might be found in an acquaintance with the issue in general of transactions in which ambition has been immoderately indulged. By this it might be perceived that the prospects of ambitious men, and the means which they used to realize them, generally ended in dissatisfaction. When the object which they sought after is obtained, they have continued in attempts to reach yet more supposed advantages, nor desisted until compelled by ruin. In reflecting upon such events, wisdom will be acquired to forego any object dictated by ambition. Hence caution will be observed, and nothing undertaken but what, in human probability, will be advantageous either to himself or others.

A man of information can often preserve himself from many evils, physical as well as mental, which injure others. In a manner far more expeditious than by observing the effects of certain actions, he may know them by previous instruction respecting them, either silently or in a more public manner. By knowing what effects will follow from a particular course of action, he may escape much injury, and practise those actions which shall be most conducive to his welfare. He will not need experience, the instructor of a large proportion of human beings, to teach him in many things, knowing, by reflection and reasoning, the causes of many distresses in life. Hence, by wise conduct, he will escape some of the calamities which men endure, rendering life a source of affliction instead of happiness, which it was designed to be rendered. Excluding the incidents of life, to which all men are subject, this knowledge will make him more prosperous throughout it, and conduct him in safety to its close. The greatness of the advantage may be estimated by observing the anguish of mind and agony of body of some men, which might in some measure have been avoided by previous knowledge.

The numerous errors of men leading to mistake in conduct, cannot be removed but by an extensive acquaintance with human affairs. Great benefit would be derived from exercising the judgment upon events and their issue, whether in ancient or modern times, which have been recorded for the instruction of men. In these, the failure of laborious undertakings might be seen to arise from having been engaged in prematurely. The source of transactions involving men in misery, might be seen to exist in the unrestrained passions of human nature, which have prevented the taking a correct view of attendant circumstances, and perverted the judgment. By contemplating men's actions, the particular errors which marked their conduct might sometimes be discovered, and which have often obscured the excellent qualities of their character. There would then be greater facility in remedying these errors, in order that they might not in like manner be a means of injury. True notions of things would be acquired by studying attentively the history of mankind. The wrong ideas which men entertain of themselves, of others, and of the design of governments, would be gradually removed. Suitable conceptions would be formed respecting the capacity of the mind, and proper sentiments cherished concerning actions appropriate to any particular station in society. Errors respecting other persons would also be gradually removed. A man who has not been accustomed to observe human nature as exhibited either in public life, or in the recorded actions of men, will often entertain serious errors respecting the character and conduct of others. And if he has studied this branch of knowledge for his own purposes alone, in a particular department, he will be mistaken respecting it in other transactions. There must be combined with it reflection upon the actions of communities; for only by frequent intercourse with men in the same circumstances, a power of distinguishing individual character for certain purposes would be acquired. Hence, a man not being accustomed to judge, from the general actions of men their bearing upon the welfare of others, would appear to little advantage when engaged in more important affairs, since he would know only what kind of character would suit him as a mercantile man. But by the cultivation of his mind, he would acquire a habit of viewing more extensively the characters of men, and judging more accurately concerning them. Thus he would become qualified to exert greater influence in whatever station he might be placed.

A more enlarged acquaintance with different subjects would, to many, remove an obstacle in the way of improvement. By devoting too little time to the acquisition of knowledge, a small portion only is acquired, acting injuriously rather than otherwise, by making such persons entertain false ideas of its easy acquisition. In this way it closes the avenues of information; for when men, knowing but little, imagine that they can acquire more with facility and expedition, whenever they put forth some trifling exertion, it is clear that but little progress will be made in it. But by more extensive study its difficulties will be perceived, and their own deficiencies, and thus greater energy and perseverance will be used to acquire it. By this means they will learn to estimate others according to their merit, and the errors respecting them will be removed.

More correct notions will also be formed concerning other things, and those mistakes rectified which have been received from only superficial views, or notions conveyed into the mind by early instruction. In the season of youth, probably, a person has heard some actions much extolled, by which one nation has been ruined, and another exalted. The achievements of the man by whose agency it was chiefly effected, and his conquests, have been exhibited in language conveying an impression to the mind, that those who act like the class to which he belongs, are alone entitled to honour. Hence also an idea is entertained that the only design of government is to maintain the glory of a nation, by taking advantage of every opportunity to extend territory and increase dominion. By reflection and knowledge it will be perceived that much effected of this nature, has resulted more in the misery of many, than the happiness of a few. Gradually acquiring, therefore, more correct notions, he will be ready to protect the oppressed from injury—to promote liberty and prosperity. So far as is consistent with justice, he will assist in the attainment of these ends, by the best means which reason and religion suggest.

An increase of information upon various topics would conduce both to self-improvement and the good of others. It would be beneficial to moral improvement to know much of the works of nature, to admire their beauty, perfection, and adaptation to the purposes for which they were designed. The more they are studied, the greater profit is received. Those who have devoted most attention to them, have still found something new in them, affording both benefit and pleasure. This has induced many to be continually employed in tracing the laws which guide the motions of the planets, investigating the productions of the earth, discovering what is useful, and penetrating into its recesses, to know yet more of that Mighty Mind which planned and has sustained all things. There is an advantage connected with such studies, when considered as conveying to the understanding more exalted views of the Source of them, and habituating it to veneration. Most men engaged in these pursuits with ardour, admire the wisdom displayed in their production, and, while contemplating their arrangement and design, look through them up to the God of nature.

Yet further, a man of information has the power of communicating much good to others; which affords satisfaction to a benevolent mind. It is a source of pleasure to such a man, to see another succeeding, whom he was desirous of serving, in some undertaking engaged in by his advice, and successful by the means which he pointed out. It would yield him pleasure to reflect that, by his information, success had been realized. But had he devoted all his attention and time to the acquisition of wealth, he might have been deprived of the exact information necessary.

An increase of knowledge will be also subservient to the purposes of human life. It will conduce to happiness, by making provision against contingencies. It will be a means of increasing prosperity; for the greater information a man has of human nature, and the best sources of wealth, the more competent will he be to become eminent in mercantile affairs. There is a connexion between various branches of knowledge, by which a well-informed man might improve his condition. By an acquaintance with domestic transactions, he could take advantage of favourable conjunctures; by an acquaintance with foreign affairs, he could escape losses which he might otherwise sustain; by an acquaintance with things present and past, he could perceive the great superiority of Christian countries over civilized heathen nations—his greater happiness, his nobler prospects, and his better-grounded expectations. He will also enjoy more composure of mind than others. Knowing many of the circumstances connected with any transaction, he will engage in it with more confidence, and await the issue with composure; whereas, if deficient in information, he would sustain losses in too desponding a spirit, and receive successes in too exulting a manner.

It is of great importance also that the moral nature of man should be cultivated, in order to counteract the bad influence which is exercised over it daily, by events which take place. It is generally felt, that what is constantly before the mind, tends much to form the character. If a man is habituated to reflect upon fearful realities, or to picture to himself the most dreadful events which could possibly befall him, he is alarmed at the least occurrence, which to others would pass unnoticed. If he constantly fix his attention upon subjects of an immoral nature, there is danger of his becoming a practiser of vice, and addicted to iniquity. But if his thoughts be often engaged on Christian morality, there is evidence that he takes delight in it, which will induce him to practise its obligations. The more often, therefore, such sentiments enter his mind, he is the more likely to do whatever is excellent, so as to promote his welfare, and increase his happiness. When, however, the mind is so long occupied with other objects, it becomes incompetent to attend to Christian morality with so much ardour as it requires; whence follows a deficiency in that important branch of knowledge. This inference is established by observing facts daily occurring in common life. If, then, more time were devoted to the cultivation of the moral affections, they would be strengthened and improved.

There is nothing of greater utility, or even necessity, than acquiring habits of piety towards the Creator, and just actions to man. Without these, there can be no solid ground for real happiness. When it is considered also that these habits have reference to a future state of existence, the necessity will appear in a stronger light. If these are neglected, and not acquired, nothing can make compensation for them. If the time which should have been employed in producing and strengthening them, has been given to the acquisition of gain, which by industry has been realized, what avail will it be, if errors are not removed, knowledge not gained, pious affections not cherished, and happiness not increased? The want of these will be an immense loss, whilst the acquisition of the other will be no gain.

Let the present system of business, which has partially caused this, be abolished, these evils would be removed, and great advantages acquired. As reference has been made to those indifferent to religion—the moral—and the religious—it will be suitable to consider the advantages resulting to each, respectively, from an abridgment of the time.

There is reason to believe that much of the carelessness displayed with regard to Christian morality, arises from men not having perceived any merit in it, because considered at a time when their mental faculties were not in a suitable state to reflect upon it. But when investigated at more favourable conjunctures, some beauties might be perceived, inducing a desire to receive it. The time acquired by early closing, would be devoted to some useful purpose—sometimes to intellectual pursuits, and at others to different subjects. The desire for variety would lead occasionally to moral topics. By the cultivation of the intellectual faculties, prejudice would be removed, so that whenever these topics were introduced by another, or met with in the course of reading, attention would be given to them;—discussion might be excited, eliciting the truth, and leading to its reception. There is not, probably, in such persons, a more powerful tendency to indifference on these topics, than in others. If all the advantages resulting from moral conduct were fully perceived, so as to impress the mind suitably to their importance, disregard to it would be removed, and a cordial assent given to all that is excellent. It is because of defective knowledge, that this error shows itself. Let the cause of this, the late hour system of business, be removed, it will be dispelled; for the greater knowledge a man has, and the more he exercises his reasoning powers, the sooner will be arrive at the truth—that without morality there can be no real happiness.

The moral would likewise gain advantage. Having opportunities afforded them for whatever pursuits they might choose, it is reasonable to suppose that they would be sometimes investigating the nature of the four cardinal virtues: this would frequently lead them to the threshold of Christianity. In their inquiries, they would see the intimate connexion between some of them and the precepts of the Christian religion, and be induced to combine both, whenever they agreed together. If this effect should not follow, a more habitual attention to the virtues which please them, would make them wiser and more acceptable to all with whom they had connexion.

The religious would gain still greater advantages. They would employ more time in investigating the evidences of Christianity; and become more firmly fixed in retaining its doctrines. More enlarged notions of Providence would be acquired by observing the accurate fulfilment of many predictions. History, recording the destruction of nations, would confirm belief in the predictions respecting them, and the mind would be imbued with stronger feelings of veneration towards the Author of all things. Thus, conviction of their truth would be received, so as to invalidate the assumptions of some, that they were written after the events. Nor would this be the only benefit, but they would make progress in other information tending to make them cultivate more carefully the affections of the heart. They would also have occasions for disseminating virtue, instructing the ignorant, and relieving the needy, which would conduce to their personal comfort and their future reward.

In connexion with this, it may be mentioned that it is the opinion of some careful observers, that there has been a gradual improvement in the moral condition of the employed, for some years. There exists not now so much immorality amongst them, as a few years ago, owing to the exertions of some of the employers, who have encouraged the growth of Christian principle amongst their agents. Whilst this is a pleasing fact, it shows that there is at least inclination in the employed to become still more moral. If there were a more extended adoption of virtuous principles, it would be advantageous to the employers, since duties would be discharged with diligence.

Still much remains to be accomplished, notwithstanding this progressive improvement. Many of them, once a week, spend their time in diverting themselves in various ways. Some of the diversions are not only unsuitable for the day on which they are engaged in, but they likewise require considerable expenditure. This would be saved by early closing, for the needed diversion would then be taken at other times. There would not be then so large a deficiency at the end of the year, as the expediency of recruiting the strength by these means would be removed.

The benefits resulting from an abridgment of the hours of business, would not only affect the employers and the employed, but also the public. It is unavoidable for the families of those who have gone to make purchases at late hours, to be disarranged : the family circle is broken up, and much inconvenience introduced. If this were to take place only in one instance, and but seldom, it would be of little moment, since but small mischief would follow from it. But in many cases a practice is adopted of commencing them at unseasonable hours ; hence the best opportunities for social intercourse are lost. During the day, such persons, being occupied in domestic concerns, are unable to promote, to so great a degree as is desirable, the mental improvement of those entrusted to them. It would be advantageous to them to be compelled to make their purchases earlier. If trade were not conducted at so late an hour, there would be no other alternative but this, or to be deprived of what they required ;—the former would be adopted by all. On the present system, however, it is put off from hour to hour, until the article is absolutely wanted, and when, perhaps, every person is prepared to use it. Then it becomes necessary to spend much time in obtaining it; the party needing it commences to procure it when there is every other facility for completing some undertaking. Thus much time which might be well employed, is rendered useless. If the only remedy for this evil be not used, it will continue; for human nature is always disposed to defer to the last moment what might be done, perhaps, more beneficially at once. It is generally found that when purchases are made at unseasonable hours, the parties are not satisfied with their contract. But by making them earlier, the grounds of this dissatisfaction would be removed, much valuable time saved, and things executed with greater profit.

Instead of the disturbed state of the family circle now seen, there would be presented a very different picture. The father, rejoicing in the harmony subsisting amongst the members of his family, would be musing in calm delight on the engagements of the day, probably attended with success; or with attention glancing over the events of the preceding day, or the transactions abroad; and the other members of the family would be employed in useful occupations. Domestic happiness would be obtained by many, who now, from the want of it, spend much time in pursuits which lead some to a state of uneasiness. If much of the distress endured by many were traced up to its proper source, it would be found to arise, in some cases, from the want of domestic happiness. This is the reason why many places are frequented in which immorality is practised ; and that much time is occupied in viewing representations which, however innocent in themselves, ought to be avoided when leading to prejudicial practices. If the inquiry were proposed to many whose evenings are passed, not in mental cultivation and moral improvement, but in vacuity of mind, or, still worse, in degrading pursuits, an answer would be returned, that no comfort being enjoyed at their own residence, they have sought it elsewhere. But if the practice of closing early were adopted by all engaged in trade, many of these evil results would not be produced. Upon this supposition, when favourite places of resort were closed, those frequenting them would be compelled to seek happiness at home.

Again, as each individual fact does not rest exclusively upon itself, but has reference to other things, so the practice of closing early, by benefiting the employers and the employed, would, through them, conduce to the improved condition of the public. In that time when the employers were not engaged in their immediate occupation, many would promote schemes of usefulness, or assist societies whose object might be the good of others, by attempts to redress grievances, to gain benefits not hitherto enjoyed, and to diffuse information amongst all classes of society. The influence of commercial men is often extensive, and when applied to these objects, they could promote them more speedily than others whose influence is yet to be acquired. By intercourse with different classes of society, they are known extensively, and have a kind of power over others, arising frequently from interested motives. He whose dealings are large, is regarded by others with apparent esteem and obsequiousness. From whatever cause this arises, the influence of commercial men is great, not only over those who are partly dependent upon them, but also over others from whom they themselves, in some measure, derive support. They may be considered as placed in the midst of a large expanse, in which their power may be exerted either for good or evil. Upon the supposition of their being well informed, the public would derive much benefit from their families, their neighbours, and, in some degree, from those with whom they associated. The families of the employers would be benefited by early closing;—there are many subjects upon which they might be informed, by oral communication from the principal. Having acquired extended knowledge by diligent study, he could impart it, with benefit to himself, to others who would be improved by it. Instruction given by him upon various matters would be more regarded. It would be received with greater readiness, and be admitted as truth, perhaps without examination. It is therefore of importance, that whatever is conveyed into their understandings be true. Habits and practices would be formed upon the opinions which were then conceived, and important results flow from them. Much, however communicated, would be truth ascertained by rigorous investigation. It would not be mere opinion given upon things of which there was no substantial evidence; it could be illustrated also by real events, and not by imaginary supposition. In this manner, entertainment and profit would be combined, and the effect would be most beneficial. Those to whom it was conveyed would become wiser, and better qualified to mingle in society. Here they would be the means of benefiting others. Their wise deportment and superior information would induce a desire in others to become like them. Besides the instruction communicated, by which wisdom would be acquired, the good example more often before them, in the conduct of those whom they respected, would influence them to actions by which others connected with them would be profited;—there are many with whom they have dealing, who are quite unknown to the principal, and who would derive advantage from him through their means.

He would be likewise often engaged in matters relating both to himself and neighbours. In seeking to procure benefits to himself, he would be also advancing their interest. In existing circumstances, he is unable to attend to them so much as is desirable, and for that reason sometimes experiences loss; but when he can devote more attention to them, there is no little probability of his benefiting himself and neighbours. When affairs are conducted by a hitherto received a fair trial. It has only been kept up for a few months, and then abandoned. Nor has it been made sufficiently public. Purchasers have not been made acquainted with it, by circulars and otherwise, and have been surprised at finding their accustomed places of resort closed against their admission.

The Linen Drapers have made several efforts of this nature, but have hitherto failed. It is likely however, that they will eventually succeed. There is more unanimity amongst them than others, and greater exertions made for effecting their purpose. There is a society amongst them making strenuous efforts in this direction, which there is reason to believe will be successful. In some of the other trades, however, there is not such a communication between those belonging to them, and consequently such simultaneous efforts cannot be made. In that particular line there are, perhaps, a larger number of assistants employed than in any other, and they hold intercourse with those belonging to other establishments. There should be societies in every other branch of business where late hours are kept, formed for the express purpose of bringing about a curtailing of them. Too little intercourse exists between the assistants in other trades, which is sufficient to frustrate any efforts made by a few in a particular locality. Certain districts should be marked out, not too extensive, and agents employed in them to effect a union amongst the assistants in the different branches. This might be effected by a very small number. If two or three only were to meet one hour during the week, still they might devise plans for the accomplishment of their object. There need not be any formal description of the evils resulting from late hour trading sent round to each individual belonging to this class in the district. They are sufficiently aware of the evils, and convinced of the necessity of early closing. Only let it be known universally amongst the assistants that a society is formed for this purpose, their latent energies would be roused, and concentrated on this point. It should be remembered that it can only be done by unanimity and effort on the part of the employers and employed. Government has no right to interfere in matters of this nature. Legislative enactments ought not to be made to enforce it. A man's property is his own, and he has a right to dispose of it at any time that he may please. It must be brought about by moral means, by the exertions of the assistants, and the consent of the employers.

The majority of employers are willing to close early, and are, in many cases, as desirous as the employed that this should be effected. But, in consequence of the competition in trade, it is necessary for them to keep late hours, in order to accommodate their customers. At some establishments, almost as much business is transacted after an hour which reason demands should be devoted to other pursuits, as during the whole of the day. At others, again, but little is done after that time, and yet it is necessary for the employers to keep open, because others in the same line do so. Both of these, however, are desirous that all business should be transacted earlier: the one, in order that he and those he employs may not have their best energies idly thrown away during the previous part of the day; and the other in order to save expense, time, and labour. Some few there are who will not agree to any thing of this nature. They affirm that they have been so long accustomed to those habits, that they shall hardly know how to employ what vacant time they might possess, or devote it to attractions which are constantly before them. Consequently they would be unfitted for future business for some time. These are so few, however, as that those desirous of succeeding in this plan need be under no apprehension respecting the issue.

Surely, then, in these circumstances, something might be effected to promote this object. The public, taken as a whole, is not so ungenerous as to require the exertions of the employed beyond a reasonable time. Many perceive the evils, and desire their removal. But when houses of business are kept open purposely for them, they see no inducement to alter the hour of purchasing. It is more suitable to the feelings of many to go at the same time with others. Indeed, it would be looked upon as a species of peculiarity, if a purchaser were to make his purchases at times different from others. The house of business would, in many cases, be scarcely in a fit condition for his reception. The employed, engaged in some other pursuit, would not feel any interest in supplying him with what he required, nor be induced to bring forward so great a variety for his selection. And yet, perhaps, this very time may, in reality, be the most seasonable for such employment, but, through custom, is considered not so.

The employers owe it to those in their establishments to encourage them in their efforts for this end. Those placed under their inspection may justly demand from them a regard to their own health, comfort, and improvement. Although some may consider that all the time which the employed can at all devote to business is theirs, because they give them an equivalent for it, it should be made known to them, by representation and reasoning, that these notions are incorrect.

The employed owe it to themselves, their families, and their future prospects, to devote no more time to trade than reason demands. It is a received maxim, that "in all labour there is profit;" and upon this principle the late hour system of business seems to be based. But surely the employed should have a regard to their own interest, as well as their employers'. Nature demands this: unless they look after their own interest, no other person will regard it. It is, however, almost impossible for them, under the present system, to reflect upon the advantage of any other person than their employer. So much is demanded of them, as to require the employment of all their time, the devotion of all their energies, and the exercise of their reasoning faculty. If this system be not changed speedily, to what a degree of imbecility respecting their own prosperity will it reduce the employed!—they will be unable to take advantage of any favourable offer that may be presented for their settlement in life. When hearing of any thing of this nature, they cannot inquire concerning it themselves, unless with some inconvenience to their employers; and if this occurs often, they are obliged to seek employment elsewhere. It is not convenient for many to be unemployed for some time, until they meet with some concern agreeable to their wishes. The consequence is, that frequently opportunities are suffered to pass by; and the employed are thrown back several years before they can attain their object. Nor do they only experience loss in this way, but the public also. They are unable to purchase of so many well acquainted with their particular line of trade as they otherwise might, and consequently obtain inferior articles, and pay a larger price for them. The wider trade is diffused, and the larger the number of persons engaged in it, the better will be the article sold, and the cheaper its price. There will be undoubtedly inferior merchandise in the market, which will sometimes gain an extravagant price. Still it must be allowed that the larger the number of skilful persons in any trade, the better will be the article. When of excellent quality, it will be examined with attention, and its value ascertained. Now, in order that a person may gain customers for this article, he will exercise his inventive powers, and employ his energies, to produce one superior in quality, but equal in price, or equal in quality, and produced at a smaller expense. Thus he will be able to compete with those in the same trade with himself, and the public will gain the benefit. Early closing, by affording opportunities for a larger number of the employed to look after their own interest with greater care, will be the means of more being engaged in business on their own account than at present; and will thus afford scope for a larger number of materials being brought into the market, and of a better quality. The public, being purchasers of these, will be considerably benefited; some, with limited incomes, procuring articles of excellent quality at a cheaper rate than now; others, of tolerable fortune, procuring the very best at the price which they now pay for inferior.

From these considerations it is apparent that the system of late traffic is productive of many evils; and that an abridgment of the time would yield many advantages. Every legitimate attempt, therefore, ought to be made to remove the one, and adopt the other. The present system makes those employed in a condition but little superior to that of a captive confined to perform the rigorous demands of his master: the one, by the customs of business, is kept at his employment so long as to injure both his body and mind; the state of the other, it is possible, may be easier, and in civilized countries is but seldom more rigorous. There is, however, this difference—that in the one case the means of obtaining liberty can always be used, but not in the other. The remedy, however, may be applied, without abandoning employment. If the system now recommended be adopted universally, the improvement will commence. Important as the class of the employed is now in society, it will become still more important, and diffuse benefits throughout different spheres of human life.

J. Rider, Printer, 14, Bartholomew Close, London.

THE

WRONGS OF OUR YOUTH;

AN ESSAY

ON THE

EVILS OF THE LATE-HOUR SYSTEM.

BY

RALPH BARNES GRINDROD, LL.D.

AUTHOR OF "BACCHUS," ETC.

"If there be anything to which the attention of society should be especially directed, it is the educational improvement of those whose occupations are inconsistent with frequent mental cultivation."—ADDISON.

"The world would be more happy, if persons gave up more time to an intercourse of friendship. But money engrosses all our deference; and we scarce enjoy a social hour, because we think it unjustly stolen from the main business of life."—SHENSTONE.

"Withhold not good from them to whom it is due, when it is in the power of thine hand to do it."—PROV. iii. 27.

LONDON:

WILLIAM BRITTAIN, AND CHARLES GILPIN.

MANCHESTER:

WILLIAM IRWIN, 39, OLDHAM STREET.

1843.

MANCHESTER:
PRINTED BY WILLIAM IRWIN,
39, OLDHAM STREET.

This Essay

IS INSCRIBED WITH THE MOST SINCERE FEELINGS

OF ADMIRATION AND ESTEEM,

TO ONE WHOSE PHILANTHROPIC EXERTIONS ON BEHALF OF

SUFFERING HUMANITY,

PECULIARLY ENTITLE HIM TO THE HONORABLE DISTINCTION

OF

THE FRIEND OF THE POOR,

THE RIGHT HONORABLE LORD ASHLEY, M.P.

WITH

THE EARNEST PRAYER, THAT (UNDER THE DIVINE BLESSING)

HE MAY LONG BE SPARED TO HIS COUNTRY

AND HIS FRIENDS,

AND ENABLED FULLY TO ACCOMPLISH THOSE BENEVOLENT

AND HUMANE DESIGNS,

FOR THE BENEFIT OF HIS FELLOW CREATURES,

WHICH HE HAS SO HAPPILY AND

SUCCESSFULLY BEGUN.

TABLE OF CONTENTS.

DIVISION THE FIRST.

THE ORIGIN AND PROGRESS OF THE EVIL.

I. Preliminary Remarks.—II. The system of Late Hours one of comparatively modern growth.

DIVISION THE SECOND.

ILLUSTRATIONS OF THE NATURE, EXTENT, AND CAUSES OF THE EVIL.

I. *The nature of the employment, and hours of attendance upon business.*—1. Domestics. 2. Dress-makers and Milliners. 3. Embroiderers. 4. Shirt-makers, and Slop-workers in general. 5. Children engaged in the Metal Manufactures—6, in the manufacture of Earthenware, &c.—7, in the Manufacture of Machine Lace, Pillow Lace, and Hosiery—8, in Calico Printing—9, in Paper Making—10, in Draw-boy Weaving, Winding, and Warping—11, in Rope and Twine Making—12, in Fustian Dressing and Cutting—13, in Card-setting—14, in Straw-plaiting—15, in Printing and Bookbinding—16, Assistants in Shops and Warehouses, Clerks, &c. &c.—II. *The general treatment of individuals engaged in these various occupations.*—III. *The unreasonable and heedless conduct of purchasers, a prolific source of late hours, and other grievances common to young persons engaged in business.*

DIVISION THE THIRD.

EFFECTS OF THE SYSTEM OF LATE HOURS IN VARIOUS WAYS.

I. *In a Moral point of view.*—II. *In an Intellectual point of view.*—III. *In a Physical point of view.* A. Exposure to an impure atmosphere. *a.* The importance of pure air. *b.* Causes of impure air. *c.* Effects of impure air. B. Peculiar nature of employments. C. The influence of a dry atmosphere and unnatural elevation of temperature. D. The influence of late hours and long-continued labour during the period of growth. E. The effects of the partial obstruction of light. F. Effects of late hours in business on the Eyes. G. The influence of the system in a dietetic point of view. H. Disease and mortality induced by the system. *a.* General feeling of ill health. *b.* Appearance and complexion. *c.* Muscular power and weight—stature—thinness. *d.* Disorders of the stomach and bowels. *e.* Affections of the lungs and air pipes. *f.* Mortality.—IV. *Incidental Evils.* A. Interference of Saturday evening-trading with the duties of the Sabbath. B. Its interference with domestic and social intercourse, family worship, and other duties. C. Its interference with the natural hours of rest. D. Its prevention of the practice of early rising.

DIVISION THE FOURTH.

MOTIVES FOR AN ALTERATION OF THE SYSTEM.

I. In reference to the employed. II. In reference to employers. III. In reference to the public. IV. Its practicability.

AND PROGRESS OF THE EVIL.

.—The acquisition of wealth characterizes the
the energies of the present generation. The
; the glory of God, would seem to be the chief
virtue, and happiness, in the true sense of the
derations. An eminent writer observes, that
the nation a universal emulation for wealth,
ll the honours which are the proper right of
Another author remarks, that " the sciences are
he physical are engrossing, every day, more
re. l that the " worship of the beautiful and good
has culation of the profitable." How correct the
rer table the results.

This unnatural state of things, is not only subversive of moral and
intellectual improvement, but utterly at variance with the principles and
precepts of Christianity. It involves an intercourse and communion with
the world which is destructive of all spiritual and intellectual advancement.
It exercises a selfish and sensual influence on its votaries. It sets at
nought the endearments of social and domestic intercourse. The man who
worships mammon is dead to every generous feeling. The things of the
earth constitute his chief good. No heavenly aspirations animate his soul.
Milton describes him as

" The least erected spirit that fell
From heaven: for even in heaven his looks and thoughts
Were always downward bent; admiring more
The riches of heaven's pavement, trodden gold
Than aught divine or holy else, enjoyed
In vision beatific."

The Christian views the possession of wealth with far different motives and
feelings. He remembers that it is impossible to serve both God and
mammon. The memorable but expressive words of the Saviour exercise
their due influence on his mind—" How hardly shall they that have riches
enter into the kingdom of heaven." In his estimation the riches of earth
are infinitely subordinate in value to the treasures of heaven. Hence his
conduct in business is regulated by the pure and imperishable principles
of truth and rectitude.

The inordinate love of wealth carries with it its own punishment. The
prize is attained at a cost which never fails to entail on its possessor the
fruits of bitter repentance. In most cases it is secured when the relish or
capacity for enjoyment has fled for ever. The possession of wealth unduly
acquired may secure the honours of the world, but it no less certainly calls
down the retribution of God. The Lord *abhors* the covetous man. " The

wicked blesseth the covetous, whom the Lord abhorreth." The riches of the covetous are corrupt. Their silver is cankered—their enjoyments are vain and unsatisfactory. Care and anxiety corrode the pleasures and pursuits of life. The unhallowed spirit of gain thus defeats its own purpose. The modern spirit of competition comprehends within its circle the great mass of the community. The man who sets his heart on the acquirement of wealth, and who traverses the earth to secure the object of his ambition, requires subordinate agents to execute his schemes of aggrandizement. These agents are in all things subject to his will. They, too, are required to sacrifice their comfort—and happiness—and enjoyments, at the altar before which their director falls prostrate. Hence a grievance peculiar in many respects to the present day, which loudly calls for redress.

Of all the evils which flow from competition in business, none seems fraught with consequences so injurious or unjust as the system of late hours. This subject possesses deep interest in all its details, and influences to a considerable extent the happiness and welfare, temporal and eternal, of thousands of our fellow creatures. Hence it demands our serious and attentive consideration.

II. *The system of late hours in business one of comparatively modern growth.* —The records of the ancients show that the traffic in goods was transacted during the more early and appropriate hours of the day. This observation applies with equal force to the habits of our ancestors. In the Northumberland household book for 1512, we are told that the family rose at six in the morning, the lord and lady had their breakfast set on the table at seven o'clock, dinner at ten, supper at four in the afternoon, the gates were all closed at nine, and no further ingress or egress was permitted. The business hours of the period were of course duly regulated by these early habits. The hours of meals were much the same in the reign of Elizabeth. "With us," remarks Holinshed, "the nobilitie, gentrie, and students, do ordinarily go to dinner at eleven before noon, and to supper at five and six at afternoon. The merchants dine and sup seldom before twelve at noon and six at night, especially in London. The husbandmen dine also at high noon, as they call it, and sup at seven or eight, but out of term in our universities the scholars dine at ten." The fashionables of Holinshed's time, as the historian insinuates, were a little inclined to become extravagant in their habits, "for," he observes, "the nobilitie, gentlemen, and merchantmen, especiallie at great meetings, do sit commonlie till two or three of the clock at afternoons." Dr. Cogan, in his Haven of Health, 1584, in some directions in reference to diet, recommends that dinner should be taken about four hours after breakfast. It would appear that it was customary to sit down to the latter meal at 7 A. M., "for," remarks this writer, "the most convenient time for dinner is about *eleven of the clocke* before noon.—In 1570 this was the usual time of serving it in the University of Oxford;—elsewhere about noon." Dr. Cogan adds, that at the same seat of learning "they supped at five of the clocke in the afternoon." About the middle of the seventeenth century, it was the practice in the metropolis, to ring the Bow-bell exactly at nine o'clock in the evening, which was a signal for domestics to conclude the labour of the day, and to repair to supper and to bed: "a bell," remarks Fuller, "which the masters thought rang too soon, and the apprentices too late." "The stately dames of Edward the Fourth's court," remarks Warner, in his Antiquities, "rose with the lark, despatched their dinner at eleven o'clock in the forenoon, and shortly after eight were wrapt in slumber." How would these reasonable people (reasonable at least in this respect) be astonished, could they be but witnesses to the present distribution of time among the children of fashion? Would they not call all the perverse conduct of those who *rise* at one or two, *dine* at eight, and retire to bed when the morning is unfolding all its glories, and nature putting on her pleasing aspect, absolute insanity? Pope says,

> Time was, a sober Englishman would knock
> His servant up, and rise by five o'clock.

Matters now, however, are reversed. The hours best adapted to exercise, whether physical or intellectual, are engaged in unnatural sleep, while nature's appointed period of repose is devoted to the transaction of business and pleasure. The dissipated habits of the people of fashion, in the reign of Charles II., did not interfere with the hours of meals. Pepys, in his Memoirs, mentions noon as the hour for dinner at that period. So late even as the eighteenth century, the nobility and gentry dined at two or three. The fashionables, however, towards the close of the century, began to dine at five. George III. withstood this novel custom, and continued to dine at three o'clock. An anecdote is told of Mr. Pitt, the celebrated statesman, which well illustrates this absurd practice. The Duchess of Devonshire on one occasion invited Mr. Pitt to dine with her on a specified evening, intimating at the time that dinner would be on the table at nine o'clock. "I would gladly," gravely replied Mr. Pitt, "have accepted the invitation of your grace, but that I have a previous invitation to sup with a friend at—*half-past eight o'clock.*"

The tide of fashion has exercised a similar influence on the meetings of our legislative assemblies. It was formerly the practice to deliberate on the weighty affairs of the state, at that period of the day when the faculties are in the most vigorous condition, and the mind, of course, is best fitted for healthy exercise. In the present day, the hours of night are selected for the purpose—a time when the system in its natural state looks for repose. The custom is absurd and injurious in many respects. In reference to the health of the members, it is most pernicious in its results. Numbers of the brightest ornaments of the senate—men whose invaluable services the country could ill afford to spare—have been prematurely removed from a sphere of high usefulness, by long-continued debates in a close and consequently impure atmosphere. The truth of this remark is acknowledged by the great majority of the members themselves, who repeatedly express their gratitude to the honourable member for Salford, who so determinedly opposes himself to midnight discussions; and yet, as he informs the writer, it is with continued vigilance alone; that he is enabled even to place a check on a practice, alike detrimental to comfort, health, or to a vigorous exercise of the faculties of the mind. The return of the "Sittings of the House," for 1843, dated August 18th of the same year, shows, that from the 2d of February to the 17th of August—119 days, and three Saturdays, the hours of sitting were $986\frac{1}{2}$; being an average of eight hours and seventeen minutes for each debate. Of this period, the hours *after midnight* occupied in discussing matters of the highest moment to the state, were $105\frac{1}{2}$; and out of 119 sittings, the house did not separate until after twelve o'clock at night, for no less than 89 times, or more than two-thirds of the whole. Even this state of things is a remarkable modification of the extremely late sittings of former parliaments, whose debates frequently did not commence until near the hour of midnight, nor terminate until the great mass of the labouring population had begun their daily avocations.

The system of late hours in business, as well as in domestic concerns, unfortunately exercises its baneful influence on a class of persons who can least afford to bear the burden of its penalties—those whose means are but limited, and whose opportunities of improvement, even at the best, are but small. The time of this class of individuals is doubly precious. The rich and the gay may, without much inconvenience, engage in the pleasures of the table, or the frivolities of fashion. Let them remember, however, that the practice of late hours influences, to a considerable extent, the welfare and happiness of thousands, who, unlike themselves, are engaged during the day in the duties of their several occupations, and possess no means of redress. The system, therefore, bears, with peculiar and disproportionate hardness, upon the character and future prospects of a humble, but deserving class of individuals.

DIVISION THE SECOND.

ILLUSTRATIONS OF THE NATURE, EXTENT, AND CAUSES OF THE EVIL.

It is impossible within the brief limits of an essay, to enter at length into an investigation of this important subject. It will be necessary, therefore, to confine our remarks to an exposition of some of the more glaring and characteristic features of the system.

I. *The nature of the employment and hours of attendance upon business.*—
1. To estimate the number of those individuals, whose character and prospects in life are, more or less, influenced by the system of late hours in business, would be to include by far the greater portion of the community. Even the *domestics* of those establishments, retail or wholesale, where this practice is in vogue, to a considerable extent, participate in the evils. Theirs' is, indeed, a life of hardship and privation. The feeling heart may well extend its sympathy to this humble, but industrious, class,

> Whose drudgery unheeded goes,
> Their joys unreckon'd, as their cares or woes.

2. *Dress Makers and Milliners* are among the most severe sufferers from the system of late hours. Their lives engaged in unremitting toil and close confinement, their spirits depressed by bodily weakness, induced by long hours and sedentary business—theirs is a grievance which calls for peculiar commiseration. These victims of fashionable life, usually continue at their depressing avocations, with slight intermissions for meals, for a period of time as unreasonable in its duration as it is destructive to their health. A tradesman, whose establishment overlooked the upper apartments of an eminent dress maker, in Manchester, remarked, that how late soever he might terminate his labours, or how early he might resume them, he was certain to find some of those employed in the establishment in question, engaged at their monotonous and almost incessant occupation.

> Alas! poor lady!
> 'Tis a hard bondage.
> SHAKSPERE.

The Christians of England, who so nobly sacrificed twenty millions sterling to emancipate the wretched negroes, surely will not fail to manifest some share of sympathy towards the no less repulsive slavery which exists among the whites at home. Humanity shudders at the oppressed condition of females engaged in these occupations.

In some houses this cruel system is conducted in a manner well calculated to lull suspicion. The shops are regularly closed at eight o'clock, or soon afterwards, and business, to all outward appearance, is at an end for the night. At a late hour, however, as circumstances may determine, the doors of the prison-house are again opened to liberate the poor victims of cupidity or fashion. These unfortunate beings are afterwards obliged to wend their way homeward, at an hour when no modest or virtuous female would willingly be seen passing through streets, which unhappily exhibit scenes too revolting in their character to allow more than mere allusion. Need we wonder, therefore, at the ruin, temporal and eternal, which befalls many of these unhappy creatures.

It is an oft-made remark, that if ladies who decorate their persons with jewels, were aware of the sacrifices, mental and physical, made to procure these costly ornaments, they would refuse to wear the produce of cruelty and oppression. May we not charitably hope that feelings like these would in like manner induce them to deny themselves the attractions of dress, however surpassing in elegance, which had been produced at the expense of toil —pain—distress—life—nay what is worse, the loss of virtue itself—in some unfortunate female? It is asserted, and the writer fears with too much truth, that inexpressible disgust at the system, has been the ultimatum to determine some hapless female to seek prostitution with liberty, rather than submit to hopeless and interminable labour and confinement.

It appears from careful estimates, that there are in London alone, in the millinery and dress-making business, at least 1,500 employers, and that the number of young persons engaged by each employer, varies from two or three to twenty-five or thirty-five, the average in such establishments being about ten, making a total of 15,000. This calculation, however, does not include considerable numbers of journeywomen, who work at their own houses. These females are between the ages of 16 and 25.

The hours of labour common to milliners and dress makers, are peculiarly inordinate and oppressive. There are two busy seasons in the metropolis. The one commences in April, and ends in July or the commencement of August; the other lasts from October till Christmas. During these seasons, and in particular the former, the young females unfortunate enough to be engaged in these establishments, are required, in all the principal houses of the town (including the time allowed for meals), to work eighteen hours per day. The combined influence of fashion and cupidity, however, does not rest here. It is not uncommon to commence the drudgery of the day at 6, and even 5 A.M., and to continue incessantly at work till two or three in the morning; sometimes indeed from 4 A.M. till twelve at night. Witnesses who were in a position freely to state the facts, mentioned to the commissioner, that for three months successively, they have remained at their irksome employment during 20 hours out of the 24.

The time allotted to rest for these white slaves during the height of the fashionable season, is not, on the average, more than five or six hours— very frequently not more than four. The following examples are cited as illustrations of this iniquitous system :—

Second Report of the Commissioners on the Employment of Children.—Statements of Employers, &c.

Miss H. Baker, an employer, states as follows:—"In those houses in which the hours of work are regulated, the common hours are from 8 A.M. till 11 P.M.: but that even in these, if any particular order is to be executed, they go on often till two and three in the morning—and, if requisite, all night; while in establishments which are not so well regulated, they usually go on till one or two in the morning, and often all night. In one establishment, where witness formerly worked, *during three months successively she had never more than four hours' rest, regularly going to bed between twelve and one, and getting up at four in the morning.* On the occasion of the general mourning for his majesty William IV., witness worked without going to bed from four o'clock on Thursday morning till half-past ten on Saturday morning; during this time witness did not sleep at all: of this she is certain. *In order to keep awake, she stood nearly the whole of Friday, Saturday, and Saturday night, only sitting down for half an hour for rest.*"—Ibid. p. f 204, l. 36.

Madame Victoire, Baker-street, *an employer,* says:—"If anything is wanted, it is not unusual to work as late as three or four on Sunday morning, or even till eleven and twelve in the day: knows that in the season the work is, in most of the principal houses, carried on from between 8 and 9 A.M. till eleven and twelve at night, for two or three months together—often later. A young woman told witness that she had at night often ' *laid down on the rug, because the time for rest was so short it was not worth while going to bed.*'"—Ibid. p. f 213, l. 43.

Mrs. Thomas, an employer:—"If necessity required it they worked on Sundays."—Ibid. p. f 229, l. 31.

Miss ————, *manager:*—"During the fashionable season, that is, from April till the latter end of July, it frequently happens that the ordinary hours are greatly exceeded. *If there is a drawing-room, or grand fete, or mourning to be made, it often happens that the work goes on for twenty hours out of the twenty-four, occasionally all night.* Every season, in at least half the houses of business, it happens that the young persons occasionally work twenty hours out of the twenty-four twice or thrice a-week. *On special occasions, such as drawing-rooms, general mournings, and very frequently wedding orders, it is not uncommon to work all night: has herself worked twenty hours out of the twenty-four, for three months together; at this time she was suffering from illness, and the medical attendant remonstrated against the treatment she received. He wished witness to remain in bed at least one day longer, which the employer objected to, required her to get up, and dismissed the surgeon.*"—Ibid. p. f 207, l. 61.

Mr. Devonald, surgeon, Great Titchfield-street:—"Has for twenty years been in the habit of attending many young persons in the dress making and millinery business. *In the busy season, the time allowed for rest is generally not more than four hours, often three: has known some who have only two hours' rest, and this for a month together.* At this time is attending two young women, one of whom told witness that she had not had more than two hours' rest each night for a fortnight. *Is fearful this patient will die.* They go on with these hours till they are knocked up: if this is continued, as it frequently is, for any length of time, the constitution receives a shock from which it never recovers. *It is not uncommon to work on some part of the Sunday: has known instances where they have worked the whole of that day. Is convinced, in no trade or manufactory whatever is the labour to be compared to that of the young dress makers: no men work so long. It would be impossible for any animal to work so continuously with so little rest.* Having closely observed the system, and taken many notes of different cases, is satisfied of the correctness of the preceding statement."—Ibid. p. f 236, l. 7.

Statements of the employed.—The young women engaged in this system of extreme slavery, themselves make the following statements:—"On Saturday night they are never out of the room earlier than twelve; frequently the work is carried on till one and two in the morning."—Ibid. p. f 208. l. 56. " If they work till four or five, they get up to work at 8 A. M. as usual. *It very frequently happens, that for three or four days in the week the hours are from* 8 A. M. *till one, two, four, and five the next morning.* It is almost invariably the case that the work is carried on all night on the night before court days. On Saturday night it is usual to work till three, four, and five on Sunday morning. *If the young persons fall asleep at work they are aroused by the overlooker.* When witness was an apprentice, has sometimes laid down on the rug and slept a few minutes, till she was called."—Ibid. p. f 207, l. 22. " *It frequently happened that the work was carried on till seven o'clock on Sunday morning.* If any particular order was to be executed, as mournings or weddings, and they left off on Saturday night at eleven, *they worked the whole of Sunday; thinks this happened fifteen times in the two years. In consequence of working so late on Sunday morning, or all that day, occasionally, could very rarely go to church,*" indeed it could not be thought of, because they generally rested in bed.—Ibid. p. f 209, l. 13. *"For a month and more, consecutively, has worked from* 6 A. M. *till two and three in the morning, occasionally all night."*—Ibid. p. f 211, l. 58. "On Saturday night used to work, frequently, *till four and five on Sunday morning."*—Ibid. p. f 222, l. 20. "Year after year she has worked *seventeen or eighteen hours for three or four months consecutively;* worked one season *on sixteen Saturday nights till six on Sunday morning."*—Ibid. p. f 223, l. 13. *"Did not leave off till three this morning; two or three young women were at that time working, and would be nearly the whole of this day, (Sunday.)"*—Ibid. p. f 225, l. 65. *"Has seen young persons faint immediately after the work was over,* the stimulus or excitement which had sustained them having ceased."—Ibid. p. f 208, l. 15. "Has known several young persons *so much exhausted, that they were obliged to lie down, either in the work-room or in their bed-room for an hour, before they could undress; they also rise in the morning tired and exhausted."*—Ibid p. f 209, l. 45. *"They often sit at work when they are so ill as to be scarcely able to stick to their needle."*—Ibid. p. f 205, l. 15. "Has known instances where, from illness, *the parties were unfitted for exertion, in which they have been compelled by the principal to continue their work. Has known this to be done in opposition to the expressed opinion of medical men. Has herself been compelled to go into the work-room when quite unfit to exert herself, and when she could not work,* although obliged to be in the room. Had seen young persons in an alarming state of debility and faintness, from excessive toil and want of rest. *Should not at all have been surprised if death had happened in some of these instances.* Many are obliged by ill health to return home to their friends every year; and thinks it very probable that of these many die from consumption. If a constant accession of fresh hands from the country were not provided, the business could not be carried on, so many being rendered incapable by it.—Ibid. p. f 206, l. 69. Often feels very faint, especially about ten o'clock, P. M.; frequently for this goes out and washes her face, which revives her; has seen another young person often faint at work."—Ibid. p. f 210, l. 10. "Began to work at seven, A. M. and went on till twelve or one in the morning. She was so unwell she could not begin before seven; but the principal wished it. Lately has not gone to bed before two or three in the morning: for a good while has been in a bad state of health; has no appetite. On Monday last was taken so ill, she was obliged to have medical assistance. Has a severe cough; great oppression at the chest; most distressing sinking and exhaustion. Is very feverish. Has become very thin and emaciated." The sub-commissioner, R. D. Grainger, Esq., in reference to this victim, adds, "I saw this poor sufferer at her home, with her medical attendant. She was in a most alarming state of illness, with symptoms of typhus fever. At the time of our visit, she was so much exhausted that she was obliged to have brandy administered in order to revive her; in fact, such was her state, that it seemed as *if I were taking, not her evidence, but her dying declaration.* It is very doubtful if she will recover." —Ibid. p. f 225. l. 34.

Humanity stands appalled at the description of scenes like these, occurring, as they do, in the metropolis of Christian England. Nor, as we shall shortly find, is the general treatment of these wretched victims much less severe than the inordinate amount of labour which they are compelled to undergo. The mere mention of the existence of these horrible cruelties, surely will induce the ladies of our beloved and highly favoured land, instantaneously to exert themselves to emancipate the less fortunate members of their own delicate sex from this destructive thraldom. Little do the fair ladies of our ball-rooms imagine, that the elegant dresses which so gracefully adorn their persons, have been made by some feeble female, whose health, nay life itself, is the penalty of her intense and unnatural exertion. Nor can we for a moment imagine the beauteous bride, with features so expressive of happiness and pleasure, to be aware what anxious toil and pain has been unnecessarily expended to furnish her with decorations suitable for the nuptial ceremony. Let us still further extend this distressing, but salutary picture. Imagine the last sad office of friendship or love, when the mortal remains of some dear relative or friend, whose spirit has fled to

> "That undiscover'd country, from whose bourne
> No traveller returns,"

are committed to the grave. Would it not destroy those solemn feelings of grief, which the mind can conceive, though it is difficult for the pen to depict, were the reflections to interpose, that the apparel by which the external indications of sorrow were expressed, was made by some poor creature languishing in an advanced stage of consumption? Reader, the above statements fully justify these heart-rending reflections.

The condition of dress makers and milliners, in our provincial towns and cities, is much the same as in the metropolis. In *Nottingham*, during the busy season, the hours of labour, in the first house, are from eight A. M. until two or three on the following morning. The health of one witness was, in consequence, "so seriously injured that for some years it was not restored."—Ibid. p. f 229, l. 18.

In *Birmingham*, the hours of labour are much the same. In *Sheffield*, the system is carried even to greater lengths. One witness states, that " the young person whose place she took had left for her health, but she died on the day month on which she left; her health had been impaired by working at Leamington. During the whole time she never left off earlier than twelve, beginning at seven A. M.,—these were considered the regular hours; very frequently they worked till two in the morning, and three times all night. *The two principals used frequently to work on Sunday:* she would not herself do this. Was obliged to leave in consequence of her health being so much impaired: she was under the care of a surgeon the whole time she was there; thinks she has never entirely regained her health; has reason to know that in many of the country towns the hours are as long, or longer, than at Sheffield. *In some watering places, during the season,* believes the young people often have not more than three hours' sleep."—Ibid. p. f 229, l. l. 42—55.

In Leicester, Leamington, Bristol, Norwich, and Liverpool, the hours of work are little, if any, less severe ; in particular during the busy seasons. The average ordinary hours of labour in these places, ranges from ten or eleven to fourteen or fifteen. Of dress makers, milliners, and bonnet makers, the number employed in Liverpool, under 18 years of age, is 1000. In the "season" they are "frequently kept to a late hour, without any additional remuneration."—Austin, Report: App. Pt. II., p. M 52, § § 288, 289.

3. *Embroiderers,* form another class of unfortunate females, whose claims upon public sympathy are in no trifling degree strong. The condition of the embroideress indeed presents a subject of poignant commiseration.

> She plies her needle till the lamp
> Is waxing pale and dim;
> She hears the watchman's heavy tramp,
> And she must watch like him—
> Her hands are dry; her forehead damp,
> Her dark eyes faintly swim.
>
> Once, maiden, thou wast fresh and fair,
> As those sweet flowers of thine;
> Now shut from sunny light and air,
> How canst thou choose but pine ?
> Neglected flows thy raven hair,
> Like the uncultured vine.
>
> Poor maiden ! if the fair ones who
> Thy graceful 'broidery buy,
> Only *one-half* thy struggles knew,
> And filial piety,
> Methinks some drops of pity's dew
> Would gem the proudest eye !
>
> M. A. BROWNE.

Considerable numbers of children, at a very juvenile age, are engaged at tambour work, in Essex, and at Bethnal Green, in the neighbourhood of London. At the latter place, a great proportion of these young girls are parish apprentices. Their regular hours of work are from 7 A.M. to 10 P.M. Allowing two hours for meals, they are kept actually at work thirteen hours daily. In other establishments, ten hours' work is the ordinary portion. At Coggeshall, in Essex, from 12 to 40 children work together in rooms which are " small, close, and without any proper means of ventilation."

4. *Shirt makers*, and young females generally, who execute what is technically denominated *slop-work*, are, if possible, exposed even to worse grievances, whether it respects late hours or insufficient remuneration, than milliners, dress makers, and embroiderers. Some recent disclosures in our police courts, have directed public attention to this subject.

In the evidence laid before the commissioner on the employment of children, one poor woman, who made shirts, states, that she works usually from half-past 6 A.M. till twelve or one in the morning. She has done this, with occasional exceptions, seven years ; sometimes three times in a week all night.—*Ibid.* p. f 271, l. 1.

Messrs. Silver and Co., Cornhill, state, that in the year 1794, they paid for making a full-fronted linen shirt, frilled, from 2s. 4d. to 3s. 2d. ; in 1808, they got the same kind of shirt made for from 1s. 6d. to 1s. 10d., and for a plain shirt they paid 4d. less. They now pay for striped cotton shirts, 10d. PER DOZEN; for printed full-fronted ditto, 2s. 6d. per dozen ; for common white ditto, 5s. per dozen ; for better ditto, 10s. per dozen.— *Grainger, Evidence: Appendix*, Pt. p. f 265, No. 738.

Mr. Davis, of Stepney, states, that on an average, women cannot earn more than 2s. 6d. to 3s. and 4s. a-week, and " to do this they must work very close."—*Ibid.* p. f 269, l. 33.

One of the London Board of Guardians states, that in one of their Union houses, " the whole of the female paupers were employed in shirt-making, and receiving one penny for *making three common shirts ;* thus allowing the master an enormous profit on the needlework."—*Ibid.* p. f 265, l. 68.

On Thursday, the 26th of October last, a smartly dressed female applied at the Lambeth Street Police Office, for a warrant against a shirt maker, who, there was reason to believe, had pawned the materials with which she had been entrusted for making some shirts. It appears that the applicant was a person who undertook to make up large quantities of these articles for the seller, and employed a number of females in the process. The contract of the applicant for the shirts was three-halfpence each, and she gave them out to be done for a penny farthing; so that she made a farthing profit each.

Slop-workers generally are in the same lamentable condition. The remuneration for this kind of labour is reduced to the smallest possible limits. " A wretched looking woman, with a squalid, half-starved infant at her breast," was accused at the Lambeth Street Police Office, before the same magistrate, and on the same day as in the case of the shirt maker above mentioned, for having unlawfully pawned some trousers, with the materials for which she had been entrusted for the purpose of making up, by a dealer in ready-made clothing, residing in the neighbourhood of the office. It appears that the poor creature, who wept bitterly while the evidence was being adduced, was compelled to pledge a part of her work when it was finished, to enable

B

her to go on with the remainder, and to provide food for herself and children's maintenance. The remuneration, however, that she received for her labour, was so wretched, that she could not procure dry bread for herself and her children. It seems that *the sum paid for making trousers was seven-pence per pair, and out of that she was obliged to provide thread to make them.* The representative of the slopseller, on being appealed to as to the truth of this statement by the astonished and humane magistrate, affirmed, that a *"good living"* might be made at that kind of work ; the said *"good living"* extending, according to the foreman, to seven shillings per week, to earn which, it seemed to be admitted, " the night as well as the day would be required, without interruption or intermission of the toil." The poor creature's dwelling, on after investigation, was found to be the very picture of wretchedness, almost without a vestige of furniture of any kind, and quite unfit for the residence of human beings.

It will be almost impossible, in the brief limits of a popular essay, to exhibit the extent of those grievances which influence the youth of both sexes, employed in various kinds of labour. A brief, and, consequently, imperfect outline, therefore, can alone be given. In the furtherance of this object, the various trades and other employments, will be classified under various heads.

5. *The children and young persons employed in the metal manufactures,* including all descriptions of *ironmongery, japan and tin wares, machines, tools, screws, nails, pins,* and the various articles commonly denominated *Sheffield and Birmingham wares,* are those which first come under our notice.

On the average, children engage in these employments at from eight to ten years of age. Many, however, commence at seven, and some even at a more juvenile age. In Sheffield, the great majority do not begin until they are eleven.

The little *pin-headers,* who are extensively employed at Warrington, commence their career in labour as early as five years of age, and at all periods from this age to between eight and nine, when they are found generally and regularly at work. Dr. James Kendrick states, that " Pin makers employ a great many children, some as early as six years of age."—*Austin, Evidence: Appendix,* Pt. II. p. *m* 6, l. 12. Mr. P. Edelston, a principal in the firm of T. Edelston and Co., says, "We admit them as soon as they are able to reach the block ; the fingers of the little ones are more fitted to handle the small work."—*Ibid.* p. *m* 3, l. 12. The same practice exists amongst pin makers in the west of England.

In the east of Scotland, great numbers of children are employed at a very early age in the manufacture of nails. Many of them are thus engaged when not older than six.—*Frank's Report: Appendix,* Pt.II,p. K 3, §§17,18.

The hours of work of these children are equally objectionable. The period varies according to the circumstances of business, or the peculiar nature of the employment. The hours of labour are stated to be shorter and less fatiguing in Birmingham than in any large manufacturing town in the kingdom. The actual period of work in this town (not including the time allotted for meals) is ten hours. From orders, however, or press of business, those children who assist the men, as in the button trade for example, are sometimes kept at work from 6 A.M. till eleven or twelve at night. The misconduct of adults also entails much hardship on the poor children, who, in these cases, are kept from 4 A.M. till 9 P.M., or later, and sometimes even all night.

In Wolverhampton, Wednesfield, Sedgely, and Willenhall, the condition of the children in this respect is much worse. In none of the different trades in Wolverhampton, whether the work be light or heavy, are the regular hours of labour less than twelve, and in some thirteen. Often, however, the work is continued consecutively fourteen and fifteen, and occasionally, even sixteen and eighteen hours. Mr. William Walters, registrar of births, deaths, and marriages, states, that "the children work from fourteen to sixteen hours daily on an average, particularly those employed by the locksmiths, and that the small masters among the locksmiths all work just as hard."—*Horne, Evidence: Appendix*, Pt. II, p. 91, l. 5. At Willenhall, the majority of adults, on those days when they are compelled to be in earnest, "work as long as they can possibly stand," and "boys, of whatever age, are all obliged to work the same length of time as the men; very often longer, because they have not the same liberty to go out for an interval of rest, or to get refreshment."—*Second Report of Commissioners*, p. 51—315. At Sheffield, when business is urgent, "the hafters' children are sometimes worked through a part of the night, especially on Friday evenings." They go to work about 7 A.M., and work till eight or nine at night. The commissioner states, that he believes that "fourteen hours would be very little, if at all, beyond the average" period of their labour.

The little pin-headers at Warrington, usually continue at their employment from half-past six or seven in the morning until eight at night.

6. Children engaged in the manufacture of *earthenware* commence their employments at a very early age. In the Staffordshire district, instances are found in which children are employed in the potteries *as early as five years*. The commissioners in their second report relate numerous examples in proof. In the potteries of Derbyshire, several were found at their labour at seven or eight years; but in these districts, children usually do not commence regular work under ten years of age. In the potteries of the Yorkshire district, as also in Northumberland and Durham, the system is much the same. The practice is not quite so bad in the west of England, as also in the west and east of Scotland. In these places, children are not usually employed under nine or ten years of age.

The regular hours of work in these districts are 12, or 72 hours per week—deducting one hour and a half each day for meals. In most places, however, over-time is very common, and in great numbers of instances, children are kept at work from fifteen hours consecutively.—*Scriven, Report: Appendix*, Pt. p. c 4, § 12; p. c 10, § 30.

Night-work prevails among the potteries in the Chesterfield union. The commissioner states, that in this district he found in every pottery a child employed either two or three nights a-week. He further affirms, that he "is convinced that this might and ought to be avoided."—*Fellows, Report: Appendix*, Pt. II, p. P 1, § 12.

The age of children who labour in the various glass works varies. The youngest child engaged at this work in the metropolitan district, was nine years; at Newcastle and South Shields, eight years; in the west of England, only one was found under ten; but in the north of Ireland, children commence their labour from seven years old and upwards. In many of these places, the usual age in glass manufactories to commence work is from ten to twelve.

The duration of work in this branch of trade is regulated by the nature of the process, which is peculiar. There are commonly three *meltings*, and, consequently, three *journeys* in a week, and each journey varies in duration from ten to sixteen, or even more hours. In the west of Scotland also the week's work consists of "journeys," which comprise five periods of about twelve hours each. This labour, it must not be forgotten, is conducted under circumstances more than usually disadvantageous to health. In the manufacture of glass, *night-work* universally prevails in all the districts. Relays of men and boys, each relay generally working six hours at a time, work without interruption during the whole twenty-four hours,—*Second Report*, p. 67—391.

7. Great numbers of children are employed, in particular by their parents, in the manufacture of *Machine Lace, Pillow Lace*, and *Hosiery*, at a mere infantile age. In the Nottingham, Leicester, and Derby district, numerous instances in proof were found by Mr. Grainger, the sub-commissioner, among those children engaged in the production of machine lace. "Unless," remarks this gentleman, "I had obtained a personal knowledge of the fact, I should have hesitated to have reported that, in this country, a child was placed at work by its parent before it was two years old."— *Report: Appendix*, Pt. I, p. F 10, § 76. The mother of the family of which the infant mentioned was a member, had four children : one eight, another six, the third four, and the fourth, two years of age. Those at eight and six began to work before they were three years old, and the one at four before she was quite two. Eliza, the infant, "has tried, and drawn a few threads out." These children were in good health, and were fine and pretty girls. The two younger sat perched upon chairs, their legs being too short to reach the ground. These children continued at their work for the greater portion of the day, and were continually reminded by their mother not to be careless or idle.—*Grainger, Evidence : Appendix*, Pt. I, p. f 42, Nos. 156 et seq. It appears that this family was only singular as respects children being set down to work at the ages of two and three. It is common, in the district under consideration, for children to be set to work at four, five, and six years of age. "The evidence," remark the commissioners, in proof thereof, "is indubitable." Some children are unable, from their diminutive size, to reach the work on the regular stand, and are, therefore, obliged to labour in the erect position. "Parents," says one respectable witness, "send their children to work as soon as they can tie a knot or use a needle." This is the case whether the times are good or bad. In 1825, when trade was abundant, children were sent to work at the same early age.

In Tiverton, Barnstaple, and Chard, children are similarly employed at almost the same early age.

The age at which children are employed in the manufacture of pillow lace in Dorset, Devon, and Somerset, is often "as early as five or six, or as soon as they can turn the bobbins." Numerous cases in point were laid before the sub-commissioner. In the South Midland Counties, the children do not begin before seven or eight years of age.—*Second Report*, p. 11.

Night-work commonly prevails among those who are engaged in the manufacture of machine lace. Children often work during the whole night, and this, not unfrequently, three or four times during the week. In the hosiery trade, children are engaged at Nottingham, Leicester, and Belper, at from five to seven or eight years of age. At ten or twelve they begin to work at the frame.

The duration of labour in these districts is uncertain. Twelve hours almost continuous work is not uncommon to those children engaged in the manufacture of machine lace, denominated "threaders". One witness states, that the hours are from 8 A.M. till 9 or 10 P.M., and sometimes later. If the trade, indeed, is brisk, the poor children sometimes work all night. Another witness says, "the mistresses who employ children, often work them very hard; has known children kept at it from 6 A.M. till 10 at night, sometimes not going out of the room, but eating their meals as they sat at work." A third witness affirms, that "many of the women keep the children sixteen or eighteen hours a-day at work."— *Grainger, Evidence,* p. f 94. l. 55—p. f 5. l. 23—p. f 36. l. 66. These details might be extended at considerable length.

The children who work at pillow lace making in Northamptonshire, Oxfordshire, Bedfordshire, and Buckinghamshire, are subject to equally late hours. Although it is stated, that the youngest children only work from five to eight hours, and those above ten years of age ten hours, yet young persons are spoken of as often working fourteen or fifteen hours consecutively. In Dorset, Devon, and Somerset, "even the youngest children work little less than twelve hours daily. Several witnesses state, that children are sometimes kept by their mistresses at work sixteen and even eighteen hours a-day."—*Burns, Report: Appendix.* Pt. I. p. A 12, §§ 96, 84. *Stewart, Report: Appendix.* Pt. I. p. D 2, § 5.

In the hosiery trade, this state of things is, if possible, still worse. In some branches of this manufacture, the regular hours of work are from ten to twelve, *exclusive of meals,* and even these are frequently exceeded. In other branches of the trade, the usual hours are 14, *exclusive of meals,* "and in all, the younger children, if necessary, work as late as the older hands." *Grainger Report: App.* Pt. I. pp. F 13 et seq. §§ 113 et seq.

8. Children also, are engaged in calico printing at a very early period of life. In Lancashire, Cheshire, and Derbyshire, instances occur in which they begin to work at this employment as early as between four and five, and several between five and six inclusive; many begin between six and seven, still more between seven and eight, and a great majority between eight and nine.

Out of 565 children, taken indiscriminately from returns obtained from each section of this district, it appears that 1 child began to work between four and five, 3 between five and six, 68 between six and seven, 133 between seven and eight, 156 between eight and nine, 127 between nine and ten, 49 between ten and eleven, 26 between eleven and twelve, and 2 between twelve and thirteen. *Kennedy, Report:* App. Pt I., p. B 4. §§ 3, 4.

In the west and east of Scotland, children are engaged in these trades at an equally juvenile age. In Ireland and in the neighbourhood of London, the state of things is not so bad in the different departments of the printfield. The hours of work are rarely less than twelve, including the time for meals. It is by no means uncommon, however, in all the districts, for children of from five to six years old, to be kept at work for fourteen, and even sixteen hours consecutively. It appeared in evidence that one child "when only five years of age, worked thirteen and a half hours daily." *Kennedy, Report: App.* Pt. I., p. b. 11, l 3. A second child, a girl six and a half years old, "sometimes works fourteen hours. *Ibid.* p. b 24, l. 31. A third, a boy, between six and seven years old, "generally works between twelve and thirteen hours, and sometimes fifteen hours." *Ibid.,* p. *b* 24, l. 31. A fourth, a boy ten years of age, "Often works fifteen hours, and often all night." *Ibid.,* p. *b.* 4, l. 14. Numerous additional illustrative instances were also adduced in evidence.

In the east of Scotland, the usual hours of employment are never less than ten, frequently from twelve to fifteen, and not uncommonly eighteen a-day. In this district, indeed, young persons work occasionally the whole twenty four hours. *Franks, Report: App.* Pt. II., p. K 2, § 6. In the spring and autumn, when pressing orders arrive, sixteen hours in the day are not uncommon. When the work requires more than "sixteen or eighteen hours," relays are furnished. *Ibid.* p. *k* 28, l. 4. In Ireland, the hours of labour are not so excessive.

In this branch of trade, in Lancashire, Cheshire, and Devonshire, NIGHT WORK is so prevalent, that "those establishments in which it does not exist are exceptions to the general practice." One witness, a girl eight years, states, that "before she was six years and a half old, she worked all night three or four nights a-week."—*Kennedy, Report: App.* Pt. I. p. *b* 11, l 47. A second witness, eleven years old, says, "Began work when I was six years old. I have worked all night; I went at six at night, and worked while six in the morning; I worked all night not long since."—*Ibid.* p. *b* 12, l. 32. A third witness, nearly nine. "I have worked all night many a time; I have worked all day and all night, too, without stopping, excepting for meals."—*Ibid.* p. *b* 2, l. 14. A fourth witness, under these circumstances, took snuff to keep himself awake. A fifth witness, a girl ten years old, says, "I worked three nights, teering blue colour, but it made me sick and giddy in my head, and I could not eat my meat."—*Ibid.* p. *b* 6, l. 14. A block printer remarks, that he "has seen a child, seven years old, work from six in the morning until eleven at night, for a week together on an average. He teered for his father, who worked him quite beyond his strength. He saw him one morning, when his father had given over work at breakfast time, fall fast asleep on the cold flags." The sub-commissioner saw this child at the establishment, and states, that "his arms were thin and emaciated." A foreman block printer says, "I have often seen children go to sleep over the tub; it is common enough now in some places."—*Kennedy, Evidence,* p. *b* 7, l. 33. The sub-commissioner remarks, "I am told by an eye-witness, that he has often seen the boys wheeling pieces almost in their sleep, when they have been working at night, and remembers once hearing a boy, coming up to the pay-table, on being asked how much he wanted, reply, half-asleep, ' Two days, thirteen hours overtime.' " A minister, near Accrington, says, "One general effect he has observed, that, when any meeting takes place of an evening for moral or religious purposes, the workpeople seem quite overborne with the effect of having been at work so many hours, young persons especially."—*Ibid.* p. *b* 33, l. 25.

In many of these establishments, children are kept at work sixteen or eighteen hours successively, "where a great quantity of gas is burning in a room badly ventilated, the air hurtful to breathe." No wonder we are told, that in consequence, they "are obliged, in a long succession of night-work, to desist from coming to the shop, otherwise they die off."—*Austin, Evidence: Appendix.* Pt. II, p. *m* 69, l. 3.

In the West of Scotland, night-work appears to be very common occasionally in almost all establishments."—*Tancred, Report: App. II.*

p. I 4, § 16. The same practice is not uncommon in the East of Scotland. The commissioners state, that " almost all classes of witnesses in all the districts, concur in stating, that the effect of night-work is most injurious, physically and morally, on the workpeople in general, and the children in particular, and that *no countervailing advantage is ultimately obtained from it even by the employers.—Second Report :* p. 72—406.

9. Children are employed in the various processes of *paper-making* at an early age. The extreme cases, however, in reference to this branch of trade, are not so numerous. Few children were found at this work in any district under nine or ten years of age. The improvements in machinery appear to have abolished the employment of very young children in some parts of England.

The regular hours of work average from ten to twelve. In Northumberland and Durham, however, " the exceptions are neither few nor unimportant, the evidence showing that the work is not unfrequently continued for sixteen hours." *Leifchild, Report : App.* Pt. II., p. L 4 § 30. In the east of Scotland, many mills, in order to make up seven days' work in the week, keep both children and adults at their employment, " eighteen hours on the Saturday, and eighteen hours on the Monday, making, altogether, eighty-four hours in the week." *Frank's Report : App.* Pt. II. p. K 1, § 3. *Night-work,* in some of the branches of this manufacture, is occasionally practised in all the districts where it is carried on, Ireland excepted. The commissioners adduce numerous instances in point.— *Second Report,* p 73—412.

10. Children engaged in the various processes of *draw-boy weaving, winding* and *warping,* are frequently subject to extremely late hours. At Kidderminster, in the weaving factories, " the hours of work are often so protracted, as to be to the last degree oppressive. It is not at all uncommon, for children and young persons to work consecutively fifteen, sixteen, seventeen, and even eighteen hours." *Second Report,* p 64. One witness states, " I go to work at five and six o'clock in the morning, and leave at ten or half-past ten at night, winter and summer ; I work sometimes at twelve or one again, until twelve the next morning, that is, thirty-one hours out of thirty-six with only two or three hours of sleep, and only one meal in all that time ; it is when we are working for the fall." *Scriven, Evidence :* Pt. I., p. *c* 115, l. 11. Another witness remarks, " I come to work at six o'clock in the morning, and leave it at ten at night, every night when we have got work to do ; when we work for the fall, I work later than ten, sometimes eleven." *Ibid.* p. *c* 109, l. 14.

The drunkenness of workmen is a source of considerable hardship to the children employed in draw-boy weaving. The workman, who has possession of the key of the shop, commences or leaves off work when he pleases, " always requiring the child that serves him to be in waiting for him : the beer house is his too constant place of resort ; here he wastes his time and money, and impoverishes his family, until the moment arrives that he must work in good earnest ' up for the fall ;' the children are aroused from their sleep, wretched and miserable, at two, three, or four o'clock, and they must go to their cold, dark, damp, and dreary work-room from such hour until twelve or one at noon, without leaving for a meal— their breakfasts on such occasions being brought to them." One boy, aged twelve, states, " I have begun work as early as four o'clock in the morning, and left off at nine and ten at night, when we have been hard on for the fall; those hours have been very fatiguing to me. I have been very tired, and glad to get home and go to bed."—*Ibid. Evidence, App.*, Pt. p. *c* 118, l. 60. A girl, aged fourteen, says: "I liked the mill best, because I only worked eight hours; now I work sometimes from five in the morning until ten at night; I 'most every week get up at twelve or one o'clock to work for the 'fall,' and work until twelve or one next day. My mother does not like to let me go, but if master wants me I am obliged to go."—*Ibid.* p. *c* 117, ll. 20, 22. See also p. *c* 106, l. 28; p. *c* 107, l. 60; p. *c* 110, l. 10; p. *c* 113, l. 3; p. *c* 115, l. 54, et seq.

Night-work is very common in Kidderminster, the people generally working, as they term it, "twelve and twelve." All parties reprobate the practice in the strongest terms, as highly injurious to the health and morals, in particular of the children and young persons.—*Second Report*, p. 74—413. Several children state as follows: "I have worked at night for a fortnight together; I did not like it; I was taken ill after, and had inflammation of the chest and fever; was sick six months."—*Scriven, Evidence*: p. *c* 113, l. 61. "I shall have to work 'twelve and twelve' for the next fortnight, as I have orders to that effect."—*Ibid.* p. *c* 115, l. 59.

11. In the west of England, numerous children are employed in the processes of *Rope and Twine making*. At Bridport, "children are thus employed very young, and for very long hours." "Children begin this employment soon after five years of age, and at all periods from that age upwards; and a smaller kind of wheel appears to be made for children of very tender years." One witness, aged five years and six months, "Has turned for the last six months."—*Stewart, Evidence: Appendix*, Pt. I, p. *d* 45, l. 10. Another, aged eight years, "Has 'turned' for two years." "He is very little, and his mother, who called him in to speak to me," remarks Mr. Stewart, "thinks that the children get 'stunted' when put very young to the wheel; 'but what can us do?'"—*Ibid.* p. *d* 44, l. 64. A lady of Bridport, who has had ample opportunity of observation, states, that "little girls do not generally begin to 'turn' as soon as the boys; she has often seen little boys of six, and even younger, who could not speak plain. *Ibid.* p. *d* 44, l. 49. See also witnesses, p. *d* 44. ll. 3, 15, 32, 59, 64. The hours of work are from six, seven, and half-past seven, A. M. to eight, and a quarter before nine P. M., less two hours for meals.

12. Children are employed at *Fustian Dressing and Cutting* in great numbers, in various parts of Lancashire. Their work is comparatively easy, "but the hours of labour are frequently exceedingly long. It is by no means uncommon for these children to work from five in the morning till ten at night, almost without intermission. (*See Evidence*, Nos. 125, 126, 127.) The rooms in which this work is carried on, are frequently ill-ventilated and dirty; besides, there is a great deal of dust constantly flying from the brushes." *Second Report*, p. 127—684.

13. *Card-Setting* gives employment to numerous children in Yorkshire, Lancashire, and the West of England. In Lancashire, the children are put to this work "as soon as they can make use of their fingers." A child, eight years of age, states, that "he works thirteen hours a-day, deducting two hours a-day for meals; making 1500 teeth and 1600 coarse teeth for a halfpenny; and earning 4d. a-day.—*Scriven, Evidence: Appendix*. Pt. I, p. *c* 121, l. 44. A girl, aged ten, states, "that she sets 1400 teeth for a halfpenny, and earns 5d. a-day." This child, remarks the commissioner, has posterior spinal curviture, resulting from the position in which she sits at work.

14. In Hertfordshire, Buckinghamshire, and Bedfordshire, children are extensively employed at *Straw-Plaiting*. Major Burns, who visited a very great number of the straw-plait schools at Chesham, Hemel Hempstead, Luton and Dunstable, informs us that they are held "in small rooms of cottages, situated generally up narrow lanes, and are about ten or twelve feet square. The numbers attending each vary from 2 to 30, of all ages, from four to fifteen years." The period of labour varies from five to ten hours, according to the age of the children. Boys and girls, from eight to thirteen years old, earn about 18d. a-week after paying for their schooling. The very young children can barely earn enough to cover the expense of straw and instruction.

15. Children are not commonly employed at a juvenile age in *Printing* and *Bookbinding*. Few indeed, if any, under ten or twelve years, are found engaged in these trades. The usual period of commencing apprenticeship is about fourteen or fifteen years of age. The hours commonly are from 8 A.M. till 8 P.M. with one hour for dinner. Previous to the publication of periodicals, the workmen attend earlier, and remain later, as circumstances may require. On these occasions it is not unusual to continue at work until a late hour, and sometimes through the night. *Second Report*, p. 133—714.

In those newspaper printing establishments which publish the daily morning papers, night-work is a matter of unavoidable necessity, at least according to the present arrangements. Few children, however, are employed in these establishments, except machine boys, who are sometimes required to attend to their duties to a very early hour.

Mr. Austin reports, in reference to the trades of printing and binding at Liverpool, "Printers of newspapers necessarily work at night, and the place of work is usually very close and unhealthy. The gas adds much to the unhealthiness of it." *Evidence*, p. *m* 48, No. 143.

16. Perhaps no class of individuals sustain so much injury from the system, if we regard their numbers, respectability, and present or prospective influence on society, as the assistants of the wholesale, and in particular the retail, establishments of our large towns. To exhibit this subject in its proper light, it will be necessary to enter into a few brief particulars.

The following is the estimated number of Clothiers', Linen-Drapers', and Grocers' establishments in the Metropolis :—

Clothiers and Linen-Drapers	4,199	Each of these 4⎫	assistants, that is	16,796
Grocers	4,277	have say 3⎭		12,831
	8,476			29,627

or in round numbers, for the estimate is not over stated, 30,000 individuals, the great majority of whom are from 12 to 25 years of age.

Some recent calculations make it probable that the assistant retail drapers comprehend 10,000 persons alone. To these we may add,

Public Houses....................................	4,400
Hotels...	330
Beer Shops	470
Spirit and Wine Shops	960
Tobacconists	803

with the innumerable male and female assistants in their employ.

c

The tailors of the metropolis alone, amount to no less than 14,552. The chemists of the same immense city are 1,082 in number, and will have in their employ not less than 2,500 youths of various ages.

To enlarge these important calculations, it will only be necessary to state, that the number of establishments of trade and industry in the Metropolis, is 77,000. If we suppose each of these to have in their employ, 3 youths, not exceeding 20 or 25 years of age, (by no means an over-statement) it will be found that *not less than 231,000 youths, in London alone, are more or less influenced for good or for evil, by the system of late hours in business !* It is estimated on good grounds, that there are in this great emporium of commerce, 300,000 youths from fourteen to twenty-five years of age.

The hours of attendance of assistants in our shops, upon business, are various.—The central committee of assistant drapers in the Metropolis, states, " that a large majority of their body, amounting to many thousands, are closely confined in business, on an average from six or seven in the morning, until nine, ten, or eleven o'clock at night, and during the summer months, generally two hours later, relieved only by a scanty intermission, absolutely necessary for the support of nature." On more minute inquiry, it appears that the period of commencing and closing business, differs in various establishments. In the drapery business, the hours of commencing business vary from six to half-past seven o'clock A. M., some shops being always a little earlier than others, and all differing to some extent according to the season. In the winter months, some close at eight, but an equally, or nearly equally large number, at half-past nine and ten. The most extensive number, however, usually close at nine. These statements refer to about five months of the year. In the summer months, about an equal number close at 9 and 11, and half-past 11, but by far the greatest number about ten, or half-past ten. Some shops, however, keep open until 12. The latter class, indeed, are not few in number. In winter, those shops that close on other nights at 8, keep open on Saturday nights until 10. A large number during this season keep open until 11 and 12. In the summer season, comparatively few shops close before these hours. Those who transact business more particularly among the operative classes, do not close their shops until one on Sunday morning. An instance, not long ago, came under the writer's notice, in which a young man belonging to a large establishment, had, what is technically called 15 checques, or, in more intelligible language, served fifteen customers one Saturday night after 12 o'clock. This instance is not adduced as one of frequent occurrence, but simply to show to what extent the system is sometimes carried.

In drapery establishments in particular, after the shops are closed, the young men are detained in effecting various arrangements. In the winter season some are at liberty almost immediately—others are detained about an hour. In the summer season, however, the case is widely different. Most young men are detained as long as two, and in some instances, three hours, in arranging articles which, perhaps up to the last moment, have been pulled about by inconsiderate customers, and also in removing goods from the windows, which are frequently not allowed to be touched until the shutters are about to be put up. In certain parts of the metropolis, and, indeed, in some shops in every part of the city, it is by no means an uncommon circumstance for young men thus to be actively employed until one, two, and, in some instances, three o'clock in the morning, for two or three months in the summer season, particularly, though by no means exclusively, on Saturdays. This practice was common, until of late years, even to highly respectable establishments. In many of the trades, as for example the grocers, and in particular in houses where inebriating liquors are retailed, nearly the same system of long hours prevails. The evil exists among the latter class of tradesmen to a lamentable extent. The young men engaged in the spirit vaults, not only rise at an unusually early hour in the morning, and retire to bed late at night, but attend at their unenviable employment during a considerable portion of the Sabbath. Grocers usually close at nine or ten in the winter, and about ten or eleven in the summer, and on Saturday nights not sooner than twelve. Chemists rarely close at any season of the year before ten or eleven; most persons engaged in this trade attend to business during the greater portion of the day on Sundays.

II.—*The general treatment of individuals engaged in these various occupations.*—In reference to *Milliners* and *Dress Makers*, the commissioners state, that "with the exception of a few establishments, scarcely any time during these long hours of work is allowed for rest and refreshment. The meals are taken in the most hurried manner; in many establishments no regular meal time is allowed; and in those in which a certain time is fixed, it rarely exceeds ten minutes or a quarter of an hour for each meal, at which some employers do not think it necessary that the young people should sit down."—*Second Report*, p. 117—632. The above statement is corroborated by numerous quotations from the testimonies of witnesses.

In many establishments the unfortunate apprentices are fed with coarse and unsuitable food, quite unfit for females in a delicate state of health.— "Salt beef," "hard puddings," "very bad cheese," "bad beer," "cold mutton, which frequently they cannot eat"—these and other similar articles, and even these "insufficient in quantity," form the diet of the white slaves of Christian England.

Frederick Tyrrel, Esq., surgeon to the London Opthalmic Hospital, and to St. Thomas's Hospital, concludes—to use the words of the commissioners—a melancholy description of the progressive stages by which *complete disorganization of the eyes, and consequent total loss of vision, takes place in many of these young women, as the result of their excessive labour,* with the following example: "A fair and delicate girl, about seventeen years of age, was brought to witness in consequence of total loss of vision. She had experienced the train of symptoms which have been detailed, to the fullest extent. On examination, both eyes were found disorganized, and recovery, therefore, was hopeless. She had been an apprentice as a dress maker, at the west end of the town; and some time before her vision became affected, her general health had been materially deranged, from too close confinement and excessive work. The immediate cause of the disease in the eye, was excessive and continued application to making mourning. She stated that she had been compelled to remain without changing her dress for nine days and nights consecutivly; that during this period she had been permitted only occasionally to rest on a mattress, placed on the floor, for an hour or two at a time; and that her meals were placed at her side, and cut up, so that as little time as possible should be spent in their consumption. Witness regrets that he did not, in this and a few other cases nearly as flagrant and distressing, induce the sufferers to appeal to a jury for compensation "—*Grainger, Evidence:* p. f 234. 1. 56

An inquiry into the treatment of the children and young persons engaged in the various trades, would involve an investigation of sickening and heart-rending details, too extended for a brief and popular essay.

The children employed in those metal manufactures in the Birmingham district, which are under the direct management of the principal, in general receive good treatment. An intelligent mechanic states, that "there is a marked difference in the appearance and welfare of the children who are employed and paid by the proprietor, and those who work for the adults," and that "the lower the mechanic whom the child assists, the worse is its lot. It would tend greatly to the happiness of the children in the manufacturing districts, if they were all under the direct control and protection of the principal."—*Grainger, Report: Appendix*, Pt. I., p. F 22, §§ 203, 205. The aggravated cases of cruelty, which are "many exceptions," are in those cases "where children are engaged by ill-tempered or savage workmen, whose pecuniary interests suffer from any *negligence which is likely to occur when the children become fatigued by prolonged labour.*"—*Second Report*, p. 79—448.

The treatment, however, of the poor children employed in the pin manufactories, "is so strikingly opposed to the general good usage of children in Birmingham, as to call for unqualified animadversion. They are, in every respect, ill used."—*Grainger, Report: Appendix*, Pt. I. These miserable infants, many of them of the most tender age, seven or eight years, are kept without any relaxation for twelve or thirteen hours, out of which one hour or a little more is allowed for meals." Sometimes frauds are committed on them, by which they are made, already in a state of exhaustion, to work a longer period without any additional remuneration. At this period they are "frequently punished: the overlooker whilst at work constantly watching them, and the least relaxation is punished with the cane ; towards evening, this is particularly the case, and the children were often heard crying by the porter." Several witnesses give a painful account of the inhuman conduct of two under-masters.—*Ibid.* Nos. 340, 341, 342, 343.

In regard to the food and clothing of these unfortunate children, the accounts are truly deplorable. They seldom if ever had enough to eat, and many of them were in rags. *Ibid.* p. F 23, § 215. One poor child says, " Has not had more than two or three meals this week ; never gets enough to eat." *Ibid.* p. *f* 158, l. 55. Unhappily this case is a mere illustration of a general state of things among this class, and much of which arises from the drunkenness of the parents. The parents of the pin headers care little about them, except to get their wages to spend in drink. On Saturday, the father and mother have been known to get drunk, and spend in one night nearly or entirely the whole of the wages earned by the toil and suffering, almost it might be said by the blood, of their children." *Ibid.* No. 340. As a general rule, even in cases where the most severe cruelty took place, the principals did not interfere effectively to prevent the ill treatment. *Ibid.* No. 329—340.

Wolverhampton and the neighbourhood forms "the district which requires special notice, on account of the general and almost incredible abuse of the children." *Horne, Report : App.* Pt. II., p. 211, §§ 125 et seq. In Willenhall, "the children are shamefully and most cruelly beaten with a horsewhip, strap, stick, hammer handle, file, or whatever tool is nearest at hand, or are struck with the clenched fist or kicked.' *Ibid.* p. Q 46, §§ 489 et seq. Several pages of the commissioners second report are occupied with the details of similar cruelties, in particular at Sedgley. At the latter place, children "are sometimes struck with a red-hot iron, and burnt and bruised simultaneously; sometimes they have 'a flash of lightning,' sent at them." The latter punishment consists in directing at the offending boy a shower of fiery particles from a bar of iron when drawn white-hot from the forge. One child refers to the punishment of nailing the ear to the counter. *Ibid.*, p. Q 76, § 757, *and other witnesses.*

The most abused and oppressed class of children in this district, are the apprentices, particularly those bound to the small masters, among the locksmith, key and bolt makers, screw makers, &c. The whole evidence adduced by the commissioners exhibits the urgent necessity of legislative interference.

The food of the great majority of these children, consists of the worst description of meat—mere offal, and the flesh of dead animals. The details as given by the commissioners, are disgusting in the strongest sense of the word.

The treatment of the children employed in the manufacture of glass and earthenware, presents a striking contrast. They are, as a body, comparatively kindly treated and well fed. This observation applies to all the districts.

Children engaged in the manufacture of lace, are in general "grievously neglected, both by their parents and their employers." "Independently of the late and irregular hours to which these poor children are subject, they are often beaten and ill-treated by the men who work the machines, when they are tired and exhausted by the long hours of labour." *Grainger Report : App.* Pt. I., p. F 8, § 66. Children employed by the small masters are still more exposed to ill-treatment, not from the masters themselves, but the machine men, whose earnings are dependent on the time which is occupied in winding and threading. In such cases, "the children are particularly exposed to cruelty." These remarks particularly refer to the Nottingham, Leicester, and Derby districts.

The treatment of children engaged in calico-printing, appears of late years progressively to have improved, and cases of corporal punishment are now uncommon. The same remark applies to those young persons who are engaged in the paper-making and tobacco manufactures.

On a review of the evidence laid before the commissioners, it appears evident that much of the ill-treatment which children receive, owes its existence to the pernicious system of late hours in labour. Corporal punishment is administered, in most cases, to children who are exposed to labour protracted and excessively disproportioned to their tender strength and years.

The general treatment of drapers and other assistants, clerks in offices, and individuals of a superior situation in life, is not, as a rule, by any means such as to alleviate the numerous trials and privations which are inseparable from their spheres of duty. The writer, however, desires to approach this subject with as much tenderness and caution, as truth and justice will permit. Do not, however, employers too commonly treat their young men, whose

Youthful minds have feelings of their own,

rather as mere machines, designed for the performance of some mechanical office, than human beings like themselves, possessed of similar mental faculties, endowed with the same keen feelings, and alike responsible to God and man for their conduct in life. It would be an ungracious task for the writer to enter into particulars. In his professional capacity, he has often been witness to privations which young men have had to endure, even at the hands of employers, whose moral and benevolent characters, to his own knowledge, have in general been irreproachable. In most cases, it is true, that the evils in question have been occasioned by the employer's ignorance of the subordinate arrangements of his establishment.

III.—*The unreasonble and heedless conduct of purchasers a prolific source of late hours, and other grievances common to young persons engaged in business.*—The evils of late hours owe their existence not alone to the cupidity of the manufacturer or seller. The heedless and unreasonable conduct of purchasers, frequently forms the source of numerous hardships, both to individuals engaged in the various manufactures, and to assistants and young persons in general, employed in retail establishments or in warehouses and other stores of goods. A few examples will suffice to illustrate the nature of this evil.

In manufacturing towns, commission agents and brokers have often to complain of parties with whom they transact business, delaying their orders to the latest possible period, either from occasional or habitual carelessness, or from a desire to obtain some advantage in regard to price. In either case, the consequences are productive of late hours in business. The broker detains his clerks, who perhaps had little or no business to engage their attention during the greater portion of the day, to write details by the first post to manufacturers who in their turn are urged to strain every nerve to execute the order in the shortest possible space of time. The hands of the manufacturer, who perhaps for days or weeks have had comparatively little to do, are thus compelled to undue exertion, both by night and by day, to the injury of their health and destruction of their domestic order and comfort.

This state of things, which is perhaps only casual at certain periods of the year, attains its maximum point in the spring and autumn, when pressing orders arrive for the "seasons," and the demands of fashion and arbitrary custom, whatever be the penalty to the workmen, must be promptly satisfied. The Second Report of the Commissioners teems with melancholy details of late hours in work at these particular seasons.

Mrs. Murphy, a respectable milliner and dress maker in the metropolis, remarks in reference to the excessively long hours common to her business, that "*a considerable amelioration would be effected if ladies were more considerate in giving their orders.*" Ladies too frequently delay their commands to an unreasonably late period, and the principal, who is already perhaps too much pressed with business, cannot persuade herself to refuse the order. Their poor apprentices thus become the victims of caprice or inconsiderateness on the one hand, or cupidity on the other.

The equally unreasonable conduct of a numerous class of purchasers, makes the employment of assistant drapers, in particular, and of all engaged in the traffic of goods, more wearisome and fatiguing than it would be under more favorable circumstances. Every hour—nay, every minute, requires constant attention to the same monotonous round of minute and uninteresting details. To this is too frequently superadded those perpetual trials of the patience and temper which those alone can realise who have been subjected to the unreasonable demands of inconsiderate customers.

was interrupted by the imperative mandate, "Joseph, turn out that tub of butter." The task accomplished, Mr. Day returned to his minutes of study, only to be again instantly interrupted by "rub those counters down." Nor did his reply, "I have just rubbed them down" avail him. The mandate was, "then rub them down again." His master, in fact, was determined not to let him do what little was in his power to improve himself. In summer, adds the unfortunate student, I could have risen and read by three or four o'clock in the morning, but to avoid the window tax my master had blocked out the light of the sun. Harsh as this conduct may appear, it is not an extreme or solitary case. Not a few masters seem to grudge their young men the employment of a few leisure moments in useful study or refreshing repose. So much time subtracted from 14 or 16 hours almost incessant duties, is looked upon as an act of unpardonable injustice, and detrimental to their interests.

DIVISION THE THIRD.
EFFECTS OF THE SYSTEM OF LATE HOURS, IN VARIOUS WAYS.

I. *In a moral point of view.*—The commissioners on the employment of children, in their second Report state, in reference to the moral condition of the children and young persons, included within the terms of their inquiry, that there are few classes "working together in numbers," of whom a large portion are not in " a lamentably low moral condition." This low moral condition, they further inform us, is evinced by a general ignorance of moral duties and sanctions, and by an absence of moral and religious restraint, shown among some classes chiefly by coarseness of manners, and the use of profane and indecent language ; but in other classes by the practice of gross immorality, which is prevalent to a great extent, in both sexes, at very early ages. The commissioners correctly attribute this absence of restraint, as the result of a general want of moral and religious training, comparatively few of these classes having the advantage of moral and religious parents to instruct and guide them. The low moral condition of the children, indeed, often appears to have its origin in the degraded character of the parents, who, devoid of virtuous habits themselves, are unable either to set a good example to their offspring, or to exercise a beneficial control over their conduct.

The parents of these children, urged by poverty or improvidence, and regardless of their health, or moral and intellectual welfare, seek for them employment as soon as they are able to earn the lowest amount of wages. The commissioners state, that when questioned on the subject, they seldom evinced any desire for the regulation of the hours of work, with a view to the protection and welfare of their children. On the contrary, they constantly expressed the greatest apprehension, lest any legislative restriction should deprive them of the profits of their children's labour, "the natural parental instinct to provide, during childhood, for the child's subsistence, being, in great numbers of instances, wholly extinguished, and the order of nature even reversed—the children supporting, instead of being supported by, their parents." *Second Report,* p. 199—4.

The girls thus employed from morning till night, in laborious occupations, are prevented from acquiring a knowledge of those duties which constitute good housewives, whether it regards needle-work, or habits of cleanliness, neatness, and order. Hence, when they grow up to womanhood, and have the charge of families of their own, they neither economise their husbands' earnings, nor, as the report states, give to their homes any degree of comfort. The natural consequence is, according to the evidence of clergymen, teachers, medical men, employers, and other witnesses, " one great and universally-prevailing cause of distress and crime among the working classes." *Ibid.* p. 200—5.

With regard to " the great body of employers, even for those who are considered the best masters," little, if any thing, has hitherto been effected for the moral culture of those in their employ. " When their task is done, they leave their place of work ; and then all connexion ends between the employers and the employed." *Ibid.* p. 200—6.

In reference to this portion of the community, there can be no doubt, that the interests of the state, as well as humanity, demand legislative interference and protection. It is evident also, that no measure of amelioration can be effected, unless it is preceded by a *decided abridgement of the hours of labour.* A wise and effective government, will, it is hoped, ere long, prompted by the philanthropic exertions of Lord Ashley, complete those beneficent measures for the advantage of our operative youth, which have been so judiciously begun.

The assistants of our retail and wholesale establishments, a class for the most part, beyond the influence of legislative enactments, whether it regards their numbers or their important position in society, possess strong claims on our sympathies and aid.

The qualifications too commonly sought in assistants, are such as to encourage a low standard of Christian feeling, if not a want of moral principle. The individual, who, in the worst sense of the word, is the best *man of business,* obtains the greatest meed of approbation, and, consequently, his services command the highest amount of premium. The results of this system are detrimental to the interests of all parties. The peculiar snares and trials which beset young men engaged in business, are of too much importance to pass unnoticed. They are more or less inseparable with the practice of late hours.

A. Traffic at night induces tradesmen of less reputable character, to palm upon the unwary and inexperienced purchaser, inferior and imperfect articles. It is well known, that the glare of gas-light produces an artificial appearance of value on worthless and flimsy goods. Hence, in numberless instances, soiled goods, pompously announced for sale at a " great reduction" in price, which it would be useless to exhibit in the light of day, are readily sold during the glare, and confusion, and bustle of the evening. The dawn of morning, often brings with its return, regret and mortification to the purchaser by night. The writer need not dilate on this subject. Most persons, more or less, can realize the correctness of the remark. He can state it as a fact, that one metropolitan tradesman, (he sincerely hopes the class is confined in number) not long ago, when discussing the question of an abridgement of late hours, stated, in effect, that he should not conform to the proposed alteration, because he was enabled thereby to get rid of a number of fancy and other articles, at their full price, to evening customers, which otherwise would not be disposable except at a considerable sacrifice, as their badness of shade, or faded or soiled condition, or other imperfections, would by daylight be too visible.

B. The practice of ticketing goods, so prevalent at the present time, among a numerous class of tradesmen, is fraught with evil to young men engaged as assistants. Many respectable tradesmen simply place the price on the various articles exhibited for sale in their windows. To this practice, no possible objection presents itself. It rather facilitates business, and removes the source of numerous annoyances, which, under the old system, are productive of much unpleasantness both to tradesmen and to purchasers. A considerable number of shopkeepers, however, in the Metropolis, and in our large towns, do not content themselves with this convenient and equitable practice, but announce a reduction of 20, and, in some cases, even 50 per cent under prime cost, in addition to a mass of puffing absurdities, such as " great bargains," " extraordinary low prices," " amazing fall," " immense sacrifice," and a variety of other disingenuous, if not absolutely false, advertisements. It is a common practice with this class of disreputable tradesmen, to attach an extremely low price, as for example, to a shawl, not intending to sell it for the same, otherwise it would be an unobjectionable procedure, but with a view to attract the notice, and deceive those unsuspecting customers, who walk in and consent to look at other shawls which are brought out for inspection, on being assured in positive terms, that they are precisely of the same quality and value, although in reality widely different. The glare of gas light contributes much to this imposture. Should the customer, however, either from a knowledge of the system, or the inexperience of the assistant, decide upon purchasing the article ticketed, the young man, if not immediately discharged (which is often the case) is afterwards held at a considerable discount. Numerous cases of this kind have come under the writer's notice.

C. Another generally prevalent practice is, the placing a mark against the name of those young men who wait upon persons without succeeding in inducing them to make a purchase. This fault, when repeated a certain number of times, although occasioned by the caprice of the customer, or well-grounded dissatisfaction at the articles shown, inevitably occasions the dismissal of the innocent offender. " A young man, of pious parents," remarks the Rev. Philip Cater, minister of St. John's Chapel, Canterbury, in a sermon, entitled the " Trials of Young Men in Business," " recently came to a neighbouring city, to obtain a clearer insight into trade. He had not been there five months, before all the young persons were dismissed from the house on this very account. And, in one of the largest shops in the same city, another individual had witnessed, within a few months, the departure of twenty young persons, of good character, and of industrious habits, from the same cause."

D. Other strict and dishonourable conditions are often imposed upon their young men, by this class of disreputable tradesmen. If an individual, for example, expresses dissatisfaction at an article, with a wish to inspect another, of superior quality, the assistant is required to produce goods of precisely the same description, and to insist, in unqualified terms, on their superior quality, and claims to a higher price, or when an advance in price is not demanded, no small amount of credit is assumed, on the plea that the purchaser is offered an excellent bargain. Even goods are sometimes purposely soiled, with the view to substantiate the plea of necessity for a diminution of charge. The real defects of articles must be adroitly concealed from the view of the purchaser, and, in case of discovery, a plausible tale must be invented, as Mr. Cater remarks, "to reconcile the existence of the defect, with the integrity and unsullied purity of the person disposing it." The assistant who, from scruples of conscience, refuses to comply with these rules of the trade, is considered an unprofitable servant, and dismissed from his situation.

E. It is common in some shops to adopt a system of premiums, a practice not less pernicious in its results. Goods, unsaleable either from age or damage, are marked in a peculiar manner, and the individual who disposes of them at a rate exceeding an affixed price, receives an increase on his salary of 2½, or more, per cent. on the advanced proceeds, according to previous agreement. These sales, of course, are only effected by means of deception and fraud. Declarations, in more respects than one, inconsistent with truth—asseverations of the superior quality and style of manufacture of an article—encomiums on its newness of fashion, and patronage by persons of respectable life—these, and other assertions of its merit, all at variance with truth and honest dealing, are the modes used to effect these iniquitous sales. Mr. Cater asserts, that individuals are frequently valued by their employers, in proportion to the number of premiums which they obtain: in acquiring which, they are said to display considerable *tact*. It is more correctly characterized as a display of duplicity, and want of moral worth.

These are some only of the trials to which a numerous class of our young men, engaged as assistants, are exposed. It is a system of fraud and deception injurious to all parties, and admits of no extenuation on the part of its authors. Trickery in trade is certain, at one time or other, to be discovered. "Let integrity and uprightness preserve me," says the Psalmist; and, in the long run, the integrity of the tradesman will be found to be his best safeguard, whether it regards his character or profit.

To render the situation of young men dependent on the extent and amount of sales, is but to encourage systematic dissimulation and trickery. It is true, that the employers in question do not make an express stipulation with those in their service on these points, previous to an engagement; but the cause of sudden dismissal is well known to those who are the victims of this silent, though effective, oppression. It is contended that the practice of marks applied to the sales of young men is a legitimate and useful stimulus to laudable industry and exertion. The natural and unavoidable tendency of the system—whatever be the motives for its adoption—however it may be disguised in the thousand forms of subtlety and deceit—conceal it as you may under specious and gentle names—like all other modes of false dealing, is pregnant with numerous evils. The virtuous youth, who at first looks upon these abominable practices with natural repulsion of feeling, is initiated by degrees into the "customs of the trade." Obtuseness of moral and religious feeling is the natural and inevitable result. The instruction of early years, soon withers and corrupts by exposure to so deleterious an influence.

It will be seen that the practice of night shopping affords numerous facilities for these impositions in trade. Its discontinuance, indeed, would remove fruitful and destructive temptations to thousands of our youth.

With a knowledge of these facts, it need not excite surprise that the fruits of so pernicious a system exhibit themselves in a way prejudicial even to employers themselves. Nay, employers of this class, who suffer from embezzlement or pilfering, must, in strict justice, attribute to their own imprudence or folly—to use the mildest language—the natural issue of a system which they encourage and perpetuate for their own selfish and unlawful ends.

The writer distinctly wishes it to be understood, that these remarks apply only to a class of tradesmen, whose practices are reprobated by the major portion of this respectable and influential body.

2. *In an intellectual point of view.*—" The means of secular and religious instruction," remark the commissioners in their second report, " on the efficiency of which depends the counteraction of all those evil tendencies, are so grievously defective, that, in all the districts, great numbers of children and young persons are growing up, without any religious, moral, or intellectual training; nothing being done to form them in habits of order, sobriety, honesty, and forethought, or even to restrain them from vice and crime."—*Second Report*, p. 201-11. It appears, that there is not a single district, in which the means of instruction are adequate to the wants of the people, while in some districts, the deficiency is so great, that clergymen and other witnesses state, that *the schools actually in existence, are insufficient for the education of one-third of the population.* In some districts, out of the whole number of children employed in labour, " scarcely more than one-half are receiving instruction, either in day or sunday schools; in others, two-thirds, when examined, were found unable to read; and in one, the great majority are receiving no instruction at all."—Ibid. p. 201-14-17.

The means for the spread of vice and immorality are not, however, so difficult of access. A calculation, made some years ago, shows, (and the state of things does not materially differ at the present period,) that, in England, there is only one mechanics' institution to 102,812 individuals, while there is one ale-house to 326 persons. In Leeds, the total number of schools for instruction of any kind, is one hundred and fifty-four ; *the number of beer-houses is two hundred and thirty-five.* The town council, in their report, inform us, that "*several thousands of children are growing up entirely without the benefit of any kind of instruction.*" "If the schools are few and empty," says the authority from whence these facts are quoted, "not so the beer-shops; and it is worthy of remark, that *in the north and east wards, where there are the smallest number of children at school, there are the largest number of beer-houses, in proportion to the population.*"—*Facts and Figures, pp.* 15-16. These are startling facts, but not more appalling than true. The necessity of an abridgement of the hours of labour, as a preliminary to a more general education of the people, is evident from the following extract from the commissioners' report :—" *Were schools ever so abundant and excellent, they would be wholly beyond the reach of a large portion of the children employed in labour, on account of the early ages at which they are put to work.*" *Second Report*, p 201-15. "Competent individuals attribute the outbreaks which have taken place in different districts, in recent times, to the prevalence of ignorance and credulity, in which, they justly state, is to be found the true power of agitators, the real cause which enables the exciters of disturbance to lead and delude so great a number of the people." Ibid. p. 201-11.

The education of the bulk of young men engaged as assistants, is limited and imperfect. Perhaps those engaged as linen drapers, and one or two other trades equally respectable, form exceptions to this rule. No sooner, however, are the indentures of apprenticeship signed, than, in nine cases out of ten, farewell to improvement. Future acquisition in learning is confined to a more thorough knowledge of the science of pounds, shillings, and pence. From an early hour in the morning until a late period at night, the same monotonous routine of duties requires incessant attention. Little time is allowed for reflection : less for the cultivation of the mind, either by study or attendance upon lectures ; no interval is permitted for social intercourse or friendly communication ; even the period allotted for meals is often abridged to the smallest possible extent. The duties, indeed, of shop assistants are, with slight exception, purely mechanical,—nay, worse, they are calculated to cramp the energies and to pervert the faculties of the youthful mind. The bud, however promising its early appearance—however careful and unremitting the attention which may have been paid to the culture of its parent plant, cannot be expected to expand into the healthy and perfect flower, if, at the most critical period of its growth, the stem from which it receives its nourishment is transplanted from its native soil into a noxious and ungenial atmosphere.

The period of apprenticeship comprehends that portion of existence, in which our young men evince the most ardent desire for the acquisition of knowledge. Youth, in fact, is the period for intellectual improvement. Is it then consistent with design, to suppose that at this important era in life, when the faculties of the mind and the moral powers not only are best adapted to judicious exercise, but possess the keenest sense of enjoyment, every hour unoccupied by sleep should be entirely devoted to the mere drudgery of business, to the utter neglect of matters of higher and more enduring moment ? Are there no after duties in life to keep in view—no destinies in prospect distinct from the concerns of the counter or desk, which require their due share of cultivation ? It is, as before stated, the undoubted lot of man to earn his bread by the sweat of his brow,—his physical powers demand it ; labour, within due limits, is not only necessary to procure the necessities and conveniences of life, but it is requisite to the maintenance of health. It is so ordained by the fiat of Omnipotence. The physical powers, however, only form one portion of man's constitution. The powers of the mind, and, above all, the faculties of the soul, require their due share of cultivation. Such also is the Divine will. He, therefore, who for mere selfish purposes, deprives those in his employ of seasonable opportunities for the cultivation of each, is accountable to God and to his fellow creatures.

What possible time can the assistants of our present race of shopkeepers devote to the improvement of their minds ? Their initiation into business usually commences at a very early period. The sons, for the most part, of a class of individuals who are unable to bestow upon their children a more than ordinary education, the termination perhaps of an imperfect tuition at school but commences an apprenticeship which usually consists in close and undeviating attention for five or seven years to the mere drudgery of business. Time, pleasure, instruction, domestic, friendly, or social intercourse, too often, indeed, religion itself, are sacrificed at the shrine of gain. Need we wonder, then, that a system opposed in these respects to christian principle,—nay even to humanity itself—should be productive of bitter fruits ? Is it not, on the contrary, a matter of surprise that its unreasonableness and injustice have not been earlier forced upon public attention by more serious consequences ?

Even if the hours of midnight were at all adapted to the purposes of study, such is the restless and wearied condition of the body produced by the system of late hours, that the mind is utterly unfit for mental application. Exertion, indeed, of the mental faculties under such circumstances, is almost certain to produce serious results. The end of Kirk White and other illustrious writers presents appropriate but melancholy illustrations.

It too often happens, however, under the present system, that apprentices and assistants are unable even to retain the limited education received at school, if, indeed, we except the almost mechanical acquirements of writing and accounts. No books at their command, or if so fortunate as to possess a select few, no time to read, much less to study their contents, their minds gradually lose their former relish for the stores of literature and science, and receive their future cast from the associates and associations which constantly surround them! The manners and appearance of some of our fashionable mercers' assistants are certainly not calculated either to command the respect or to excite the esteem of those with whom they come in contact. The outward exterior, however, of the frivolous and foppish shop youth, but exhibits the condition of the inner man Let our youths be influenced by a more elevated scale of morals ; let them possess the advantages of an education more suited to their scale in society, and the objectionable manners under consideration will soon disappear. The moral and intellectual condition of our young men is not so much their crime as their misfortune. It is but the natural and unavoidable issue of the system. A sacrifice offered to the Moloch of gain.

One or two appropriate examples will serve to exhibit this subject in a more forcible light. At a meeting held in Manchester, November, 1837, in furtherance of the desirable object of closing all retail shops at an earlier hour, a respectable and influential tradesman of that town stated, that he had served his apprenticeship under a master who had left one part of his character deeply engraved on his grateful recollection—a consideration for the welfare and comfort of those in his employ, manifested, among other ways, in the permission to close business at eight o'clock at night. Those hours, he added, thus gained, had been to him the source of all the improvement and advantage that rendered his more mature life happier than otherwise it could have been, and made him desirous to extend to others that advantage which he had enjoyed in his youth. The writer may add, that the individual in question, after a brief but successful career, has retired from the pursuits of business, and is at the present period pursuing his studies at one of our universities, with a view to enter into the sacred office of the ministry. This interesting record, however, does not comprehend the whole case. About fourteen years previous to the time when the above statement was made, the same gentleman took into his service a raw youth from a Sunday school. He permitted him to conclude the labours of the day at eight o'clock in the evening, and not only offered to him the use of his own library, but agreed to purchase any books he might want, provided that he would study them under his roof. The youth had both gratitude and a desire of self-improvement. Now, and for several years, observed his kind master, he has been one of the most highly honoured labourers in the South Sea Missions, reflecting credit on the society that sent him, and promoting the glory of God by spreading the truths of Christianity in those islands. The writer can substantiate the latter statement, from a personal knowledge of the facts.

The editor of one of the Manchester papers stated at the same meeting, that when in Glasgow, his master had permitted him to use for his own improvement, the evening hours after seven, and that those hours, in the period from seventeen to nineteen years of age, were to him the most profitable of his life. He had also at his command the hours from six or seven till nine in the morning, and he laid in at that period a greater stock of substantial knowledge, than he had ever been able to acquire in his subsequent progress through life.

The young men of Manchester, engaged in the retail trade, in 1837, thus represented this portion of their grievance: "We are precluded from the enjoyment of that relaxation which the mental as well as the corporeal faculties require; and we painfully deplore our utter inability to partake of those means of educational improvement afforded to other young men, in the Athenæum, the Mechanics' Institution, and other similar places, where important instruction is presented in the most attractive form, and rendered to others easily accessible." The result of an agitation of the subject in Manchester, in 1837, induced a great proportion of the respectable tradesmen of that town, to close their shops at eight o'clock at night. How then did the young men employ the leisure thus extended to them by a partial relaxation of the system? Did they evince the sincerity of their professions by connecting themselves with any of the institutions named in their address? "On this subject," writes a gentleman who had taken much interest in the question, January, 1838, "I have made every possible inquiry. They have not become less attentive to the interests of their employers; they have not formed habits of dissipation, they have not in any way degraded their characters. The reverse is the fact. Many of the young men have, I am informed, joined the Mechanics' Institution; and I am assured, upon unquestionable authority, that upwards of one hundred of them had, some time ago, become subscribers to the Athenæum. As far, therefore, as it has been possible to try the change, it has been tried; and as far as the trial has been made, it has hitherto been productive of nothing but advantage. No pretext then remains for the preventing the change from becoming universal." This communication, it is proper to observe, was written in less than three months after the publication of the young men's address. The boon, in fact, was no sooner granted, than honourable advantage was taken of the privileges which it afforded, and there is every reason to suppose, that but for the mistaken cupidity of narrow minded tradesmen, who soon broke through the regulation, the accession of members to the institutions named would have been general.

One of the most intelligent and influential members of the Metropolitan assistant drapers, in a communication dated February, 1843, makes the following corroborative statement: "the number of assistant shopkeepers that attend Literary Institutions, must be very small, from the fact of their not being able to leave business in time to avail themselves of the advantages which they offer. This I know, from painful experience, having myself joined the Westminster Institution about four years ago, but after remaining in connection with it for about two years, I most reluctantly withdrew myself, finding that it was impossible to attend more than once in every six lectures, and being totally unable to connect myself with even one class. I give my own experience, believing it to be the case with hundreds of others, who would most gladly join such institutions were it in their power."

It cannot then be said that assistants, as a body, display no wish to improve their intellectual condition. On the contrary, they evince an anxious desire to attain useful knowledge. The present system, however, of late hours in business, debars them from its acquirement. Its continuance renders it in vain for us to look for a future race of tradesmen more elevated in their views, or possessed of enlarged capabilities. Excluded from participation in that rapid diffusion of knowledge which characterizes the present era, when engaged in business on their own account, they will be unfit to mix with their equals in society. Intercourse with low and vulgar associates, the usual and natural resource, and the consequent acquirement of irregular habits, will still further disgrace their character and mar their prospects. Nor need we trace their subsequent ruinous career. The swollen list of bankrupt tradesmen unfolds a fearful tale.

At a public meeting mentioned above, held in Manchester, in 1837, Mr. Petty, a most respectable and influential tradesman, stated, that many shopkeepers in that town had been debarred in their youth from the advantages then sought to be accorded. He knew one individual who, within his own recollection, had been an assistant in a shop, and who was now probably worth £200,000. Such was that gentleman's feeling on the deficiency under which he must naturally labour, when he found himself likely to occupy a higher station in society, that he determined, and put in force his determination, to rise at five o'clock, in order to read and cultivate his mind.

The reward of honourable and successful industry, is too often blighted by deficiencies in education. Rich and influential individuals, in particular in our large manufacturing towns, the architects of their own fortunes, have not unfrequently deeply to lament the disadvantages which inevitably arise from neglect of early education. With painful consciousness they deplore deficiencies which preclude equal intercourse with those among whom in after life they mingle. Their usefulness is paralyzed or rendered feeble, because not strengthened or directed by a salutary and judicious education. The possession of wealth may secure the luxuries of life and admission into society—it cannot, however, elicit that solid respect which alone springs from superior intelligence and principle. This subject acquires increased importance, when it is remembered that whether in the Metropolis, or in the leading cities of the British Empire, the chief personages in wealth or influence, have in early life commenced their career as assistants behind the counter, or in the warehouse.

The being debarred for a limited or more extended period, from attendance at lectures, and other sources of instruction, does not constitute the sole evil of the system under consideration. Sad experience demonstrates, that the mind when long engaged without intermission, in inferior pursuits, loses its relish or inclination for reading or study. The keen aspirations of youth after knowledge, soon disappear before the pleasures of sense, and the pernicious enticements of low associates. The powers of the mind, like the functions of the body, require their due proportion of exercise. It is impossible for them to remain quiescent. If they do not advance in the scale of improvement, in exact proportion they retrograde and grow weak. Hence that incapacity, as well as want of relish, which manifests itself, after neglect of education in early years, at an advanced period of life.

A Fellow of the Statistical Society, a friend of the writer's, from a cursory inquiry, writes as follows :—" The attendance of shopkeepers at

E

Mechanics' Institutions is almost none at all. I looked at the books of the great Institute, Southampton Buildings,—it is under 5 per cent. of other people, considerably—perhaps 2 or 3." It appears from the annual report of the Mechanics' Institution, Manchester, that out of 1092 members, only 71 are classified as "shopkeepers and other assistants." Of these, 365 were between 14 and 21 years of age, and 676 above 21. From the writer's personal investigation of the books of the institution, he believes, that of the 71 individuals so classified, not 12 of that number either belong to retail establishments, such as linen drapers or grocers, or are enabled to take advantage of the privileges of the institution.

These are startling facts, and require the attentive consideration of all who regard the moral and intellectual elevation of our youth.

The influence of pure air on the mental faculties, has of late excited much attention ; Dr. Combe, in his valuable work on Physiology, remarks on this subject as follows :—" When I called to mind the freshness and alacrity with which, when at school, our morning operations were carried on, the gradual approach to languor and yawning which took place as the day advanced, and the almost instant resuscitation of the whole energies of mind and body that ensued on our dismissal, I could not help thinking that, even after making every necessary deduction for the mental fatigue of the lessons, and the inaction of body, a great deal of the comparative listlessness and indifference, was owing to the continued inhalation of an air too much vitiated to be able to afford the requisite stimulus to the blood, on which last condition the efficiency of the brain so essentially depends. This became the more probable on recollecting the pleasing excitement occasionally experienced for a few moments, from the rush of fresh air which took place when the door was opened to admit some casual visitor." Few persons but have experienced the sensations described by this well-known writer. The accuracy of the above remarks were confirmed by an experiment made by an intelligent teacher in Edinburgh. At the recommendation of Dr. Combe, he paid much attention to ventilation, and permitted his pupils to play in the open air for ten minutes, at the end of the first hour. During this period the door and windows were thrown open, and the air was of course renewed. " The effects of this proceeding" remarks Dr. Combe, " during last winter, was a marked increase in the mental activity and attention of the pupils, greater pleasure and success in the exercises, and a striking diminution in the number of absentees from sickness. The latter effect was so marked, that some of the parents observed the improved health of their children, without being aware to what it was due." An identical instance is related in the Quarterly Journal of Education for October, 1834.

These conclusive facts exhibit the influence which confinement, in an impure atmosphere, exercises upon the mental faculties. The condition of apprentices and assistants in our linen drapers, and other similar establishments, is yet more pernicious, whether it relates to the nature of their avocations, or to the prolonged period of confinement and exposure to noxious air.

3. *In a physical point of view.*—It will be impossible to enter at length into this important section. Details, therefore, will be confined to those evils which are most prominent.

A. *Exposure to an impure atmosphere.*—Exposure to an impure and deleterious atmosphere, for a considerable period, is an unavoidable consequence of the system of late hours. The consideration of this subject involves a discussion of several points.

a. The importance of pure air. An examination of the structure and functions of the lungs, demonstrates the importance of pure air. The lungs, for the most part, are composed of a vast number of minute air cells. In infancy these air cells do not exceed the $\frac{1}{140}$ part of an inch—in adults, they they are about $\frac{1}{100}$ part of an inch in diameter. Hale, calculates the united amount of their surface at 20,000 square inches. Keill, estimates the number of air vesicles as 174,000,000. Munro, states their united surface as equal to 30 times the surface of the body.

It is well ascertained that the air vessels of the lungs present the most active absorbing surface of the human body. The lining membrane of the air cells is of the finest and most delicate description imaginable. The air —and of course any noxious ingredients, suspended in the atmosphere, has free and immediate access to the blood. The heart, or central machine of circulation, lies contiguous to the lungs, so that poisonous substances suspended in the atmosphere, soon exercise their deadly influence. The lungs also are in close and immediate contact with the central masses of the nervous system, with which, in fact, there is direct communication by means of large and important nerves. Hence, remarks Dr. Southwood Smith, a single inspiration of concentrated prussic acid, kills with the rapidity of a stroke of lightning. So rapid is the transmission of substances, by means of pulmonary absorption, that the urine of individuals who merely pass through a room recently painted, receives the odour of the turpentine. The vapour of the turpentine is received into the lungs, and transmitted into the circulation with the inspired air. It is principally in this way that fevers are produced by the exhalations of marshes, and in particular from the confined and impure air of ill-ventilated apartments.

The atmosphere, in its ordinary state, consists of pure air, aqueous vapour, and carbonic acid gas. Pure air consists of azote and oxygen in definite and fixed proportions. Oxygen, however, is the only gas, strictly speaking, essential to the support of life.

In agricultural districts, an admirable atmospheric equilibrium is maintained, in accordance with obvious and wonderful design. The air which is inspired in the act of breathing, loses a portion of its oxygen and azote. The oxygen of the atmosphere, is replaced by the carbonic acid evolved in the changes which the blood undergoes in the process of animalization. Carbonic acid, in proper proportions, is the natural food of vegetables—at least during the day. Plants, however, give off an amount of oxygen, which counterpoizes the respiration of the animal kingdom.

The importance and value of pure air, will be further seen from the following facts:—The volume of air ordinarily present in the lungs, is nearly twelve pints. The lungs receive one pint of air at each ordinary inspiration, and expel nearly one pint of air during the same period. The whole volume of air in the lungs, is decomposed in the space of time required for the circuit of the blood. The whole volume of air decomposed in twenty-four hours, is 221,882 cubic inches. Fifty-seven hogsheads of air flow to the lungs every twenty-four hours. Twenty-four hogsheads of blood are presented to the lungs in the same space of time to receive the action of the above air.

The action of pure air on the blood is essential to health. "All physiologists," remarks Dr. Combe, "are agreed as to the fact, that the arterialization of the blood in the lungs, is essentially dependent on the supply of oxygen contained in the air in which we breathe, and that air is fit or unfit for respiration in exact proportion as its quantity of oxygen approaches to, or differs from, that contained in pure air." Hence, oxygen is often denominated the *vital air*, because it is necessary to existence.

The chyle or nutritious fluid extracted from the food, is conveyed by the absorbent vessels from the stomach to the lungs, to receive those essential changes, *by contact with pure air*—which converts it from dark to crimson—from impure to healthy blood—in other words, which enables the blood to produce healthy bones, muscles, and what is of the greatest value—*healthy action of the organs.* The healthy action of the organs, however, mainly depends on the circumstances under consideration. It cannot exist independently of exercise and pure respiration. The air which we breathe, therefore, is for health or disease—for life or for death.

Mr. Thackrah, in his able and valuable work on the *Effects of Trades and Employments*, remarks, "Shopkeepers injure health, not by direct attacks—not by the introduction of injurious agents, but by withholding the pabulum of life—a due supply of that pure fluid, which nature designed as food for the constitution. Be it remembered, that man subsists upon the air, more than upon his meat and drink. Numerous instances might be adduced of persons existing for months and years, on a very scanty supply of aliment, but it is notorious that no one can exist an hour without a copious supply of air. The atmosphere which shopkeepers breathe is contaminated and adulterated ; air, with its vital principles, so diminished that it cannot decarbonize the blood, nor fully excite the nervous system. Hence, shopkeepers are pale, dyspeptic, and subject to affections of the head. They often drag on a sickly existence, die before the proper time of life, and leave a progeny like themselves." The shopkeepers, in fact, almost equally suffer with their unfortunate assistants.

The relative value of pure air and food may be estimated by this fact. When human beings, from accident or disease, have been deprived of food, they will, on an average, exist for fourteen days—from eleven to nineteen days is the result of observation. Let an individual, however, be supplied with the grosser aliments in abundance, and *completely* deprived of air, and one minute suffices to terminate his existence. "Hence," remarks Dr. Farre, "the relative value of food through the organs of supply, to sanguinification effected in the lungs by pure atmospheric air, is as the value of one minute to fourteen days, and the deterioration of the atmosphere in which human beings are working, produces a deleterious effect in proportion to that deterioration."

b. Causes of Impure Air.—These are numerous, in particular in the confined apartments of certain of our manufactories and retail shops. Of late years important improvements have taken place in this respect.

Animal Effluvia, as, for instance, those exhalations from the lungs and skin, which never cease to go on at all times, and in every season of the year, and long exposure to which in crowded rooms is extremely pernicious. The air of sleeping apartments, in particular when ill-ventilated and occupied by several individuals, as most persons must perceive, emits an unpleasant odour. It is, in fact, saturated with injurious particles. The skin, even at the lowest estimate, removes from the system not less than twenty ounces of waste matter every twenty-four hours. The exhalation from the lungs is also copious and perpetual. This process is, in fact, one of the main outlets of waste matter from the system. "The air which we breathe," says Dr. Combe, "is thus vitiated, not only by the subtraction of its oxygen, and the addition of carbonic acid, but also by animal effluvia, with which it is loaded when returned from the lungs. In some individuals, this last source of impurity is so powerful, as to render their vicinity offensive, and even insupportable to the by-standers; and it is its presence which gives the disagreeable sickening smell to crowded rooms."

The air, when more or less saturated with particles of dust, is rendered highly injurious.—The lungs sustain injury in many shops and warehouses, in particular during the summer, by the contact of myriads of particles of dust, often invisible to the naked eye, emitted either from the disturbance of goods offered for sale, or by the continual passage of individuals over the floors of the establishment. In some shops, the air is literally saturated with these injurious atoms. Certain descriptions of goods also emit a most unpleasant effluvia.

The same remarks apply with equal force to many workshops, and in particular to certain trades. The mortality among the *grinders*, at Sheffield, from this cause, is truly fearful. The air of the rooms in which the process of *scouring* is carried on in the Potteries, is filled with finely pulverized flint, and its inhalation proves nearly as fatal as that of the grinding-stones of Sheffield. *Second Report of Commiss.* p. 108. 595. Dr. Holland informs us, that girls who work at hair-seating, are liable to pulmonary complaints, cough, difficulty of breathing, and many of the symptoms of consumption, of which they often die. He attributes these bad effects to the confinement, and the inhalation of fine dust. *Ibid.* p. 105—500. It would be easy to adduce numerous additional examples.

The consumption of vital air by artificial lights, forms another fruitful source of impure air in shops.—Dr. Combe correctly asserts, that a single gas burner will consume more oxygen, and produce more carbonic acid to deteriorate the atmosphere of a room, than six or eight candles. In most respectable establishments, there are not less than 14 burners. In many shops there are as many as 30, 40, and 50 burners, and in some, a much greater number. Unless, therefore, these shops be well ventilated, which as at present constructed is almost impossible, the air soon becomes deprived of a considerable amount of its oxygen, and, of course, health suffers in exact proportion.

The changes effected by respiration, form the chief source of impure air in ill-ventilated apartments.—Pure air when *in*spired, is loaded with oxygen; when *ex*pired, it is charged with carbonic acid. A simple experiment will render this fact manifest. Let an individual breathe through a tube, into a vessel containing a solution of lime. The carbonic acid expired will immediately unite with the lime, and form carbonate of lime, a white powder, which resembles chalk, both in its appearance and its properties. The experiment may be determined in another way. Place a vessel, containing lime-water, in the open air, and another filled with the same solution, in a lecture room crowded with individuals, for two or three hours, or even less space of time. The rapid formation of carbonate of lime, in the latter instance, compared with the former, will exhibit the comparative existence of carbonic acid in the two atmospheres.

Chemical analysis proves the same fact. 100 parts of atmospheric air, are composed of 79 parts of azote, and 21 of oxygen, and a small proportion of carbonic acid, not exceeding half a grain per cent. If, however, this portion of air be respired until it is no longer able to sustain animal life, it is found, on examination, to consist of 77 parts of azote, and 23 of carbonic acid. In other words, the oxygen or vital air disappears, and its place is supplied by a gas which is destructive to animal existence. Respiration, then, alters the chemical constitution of the atmosphere.

On the average, individuals breathe from 14 to 20 times in a minute. During the same space of time they inhale from 14 to 40 cubic inches of air at each inspiration. If we calculate the consumption of air at 30 inches, which is not an over-estimate, and the rate of inspirations as 15, it will be found that a single individual consumes 450 inches of air, in respiration, in one minute. During the same period, 24 cubic inches of oxygen are abstracted from the air, and replaced by an equal amount of carbonic acid. "In the course of one hour," observes Dr. Combe, "one pair of lungs will, at a low estimate, vitiate the air by the subtraction of no less than 1440 cubic inches of oxygen, and the addition of an equal number of carbonic acid, thus constituting a source of impurity which cannot be overlooked."

The experiments of Leblanc upon vitiated atmospheres, contribute much to elucidate this subject. Saussure shows that the air in its normal condition, contains from 3 to 6 parts of carbonic acid in 10,000. Leblanc (Ann. de Chim., V. 223) not long ago made a careful analysis of the amount of carbonic acid in crowded rooms, theatres, and cities. The air of one of the wards in the hospital, La Pitie, which had 54 patients, contained $\frac{3}{1000}$ of CO_2, that is, five times the proportion contained in the air, in it normal state. The quantity of air contained in a ward, at Salpetriere, under similar circumstances, was $\frac{8}{1000}$. One per cent. of carbonic acid was found in Dumas's class-room, after a lecture of one hour and a half, where 900 individuals were present. The same amount of oxygen had disappeared. Leblanc considers the presence of 1 per cent. of carbonic acid as a maximum quantity for safety, and in this case, urges the necessity of better ventilation. Professor R. D. Thomson remarks, that this result agrees with experiments made in this country. Leblanc has seen death produced by the presence of 3 per cent. of carbonic acid in the atmosphere, when the air has been deteriorated by burning charcoal. He also found that the light of a candle was extinguished in air which contained $4\frac{1}{2}$ or 6 per cent. of carbonic acid. "In such an atmosphere," observes Dr. R. D. Thomson, "life may be kept up for some time, but respiration is oppressive, and the animal is affected with very great uneasiness. Air expired from the lungs contains about 4 per cent. of carbonic acid, and hence the atmosphere is noxious. Even 3 per cent. in the atmosphere killed a bird, and yet we have seen statements which affirmed that upwards of 3 per cent. had been detected in London theatres. All these facts are pregnant with importance in reference to health. Our miners may not be suffocated by fire-damp explosions, but we should remember, that their constitutions may be poisoned by the respiration of tainted atmospheres."

c. *Effects of Impure Air.*—Few persons who have visited shops during the night, lit up with gas, and crowded with customers ; and in particular, those shops which are limited in their dimensions, but must have felt the almost overwhelming sensations produced by a change from the pure air of the exterior to a confined and vitiated atmosphere. What emotions of pleasure have been experienced after even a brief stay in these unwholesome abodes, on again emerging into a purer medium! And yet the shop assistants of our populous cities, are exposed to this deleterious atmosphere, for 12, and even 15 hours every day.

The lot of thousands of our youth employed in various manufactures is, however, much worse. The medical report submitted to the inspection of the commissioners states, that "more evil consequences to health perhaps arise from the workshops, than from the processes carried on in them." The sub-commissioner adds, that all his inquiries induce him entirely to concur in this statement. "The almost total absence of effectual ventilation, the consequent contamination of the air, the excessive heat at one time and cold at another, are prolific sources of disease.—*Second Report, p,* 100—562.

It is useless to urge in respect to this system, that use becomes second nature. The supposition is not only opposed to experience, but to the laws of the animal economy. Impure air is, in its effects on the system, a *poison*—and a poison too, as fatal to the human frame as others, in proportion to the virulence of its nature, and the length of time it is breathed. Its operation may, even to the niceness of sense, be silent and almost imperceptible, but in the long run, it is not less fatal and deadly in its effects on the constitution. A slow poison it is true—but a poison is not the less such, because it does not instantaneously work its fearful changes. The aggregate of slow changes produced by some poisons, is not less destructive than the immediate and more glaring influence of others more potent in their effects. The evils, however, of the former, ought to excite the most suspicion, because, from their insidious character, they are apt to be overlooked until, alas, the danger becomes too apparent. "The influence of impure air," remarks Dr. Combe, "is not less positive, or ultimately less subversive of health, from being slow and insidious in its progress." Dr. Dick, in his valuable work on the Improvement of Society by the Diffusion of Knowledge, remarks, "Air, when contaminated by breathing, by fires or candles, operates as a slow poison, and gradually undermines the human constitution, yet nothing is less attended to in the economy of health by the great majority of mankind. Because air is an invisible substance, and makes little impression on the organs of sense, they seem to act as if it had no existence. And although the effects of impure air may not be sensibly felt, it gradually preys upon the constitution, and often produces incurable asthmas, fevers, consumptions, and other dangerous disorders, which are frequently imputed to other causes."

The respiration of impure air, as an inevitable consequence, generates impure blood, and the health of the system, of course, mainly depends on the pure condition of the circulating fluid. It is impossible, therefore, for young men to maintain a healthy condition, either of body or mind, who breathe for so many hours in the day, an atmosphere like that under consideration. The lungs, unlike the stomach, are not endowed with an omni-digestive power. The latter organ exercises its functions on an almost unlimited variety of animal and vegetable matter. One element alone—oxygen—can maintain the vitality of the organs of respiration. This element, too, enters into the composition of the atmosphere, in a fixed and definite proportion. If this proportion, from whatever cause, is either diminished or withheld, the most serious consequences ensue. The action of the lungs becomes impeded, and the heart and circulation suffer in exact ratio.

It has been the writer's lot, in his professional capacity, to witness, on a large scale, the changes produced on the systems of our young men, by late hours and an impure atmosphere. He has often beheld, with pain, the ruddy countenance, and the glow of health, and the consequent cheerfulness produced by a residence in the country, gradually give place to pale and emaciated features, and a countenance expressive of anxiety and bodily depression. In these cases, he has invariably recommended a residence for a few weeks in the country. Removed from a deleterious atmosphere, a decided change soon manifests itself. The lungs recover their wonted tone—the blood undergoes its essential changes—and the benefits of a pure circulation of the vital fluid, soon exhibit themselves in a speedy restoration to health. A return, however, to the same polluted atmosphere, brings with it a recurrence of the former evils. The writer has over and again witnessed the pallid cheek, and the emaciated form, follow this change, until consumption, that fell-monster of our youth, has seized, with unerring precision, on its hapless victims.

In reference to the poor dress makers, Sir James Clarke, Bart., Physician to the Queen, says, "I have found the mode of life of these poor girls such as no constitution could long bear. Worked from six in the morning till twelve at night, with the exception of the short interval allowed for their meals, in close rooms, and passing the few hours allowed for rest in still more close and crowded apartments :—a mode of life more completely calculated to destroy human health could scarcely be contrived, and this at a period of life when exercise in the open air, and a due proportion of rest, are essential to the development of the system." Grainger, Evidence : p. f 232, l. 36.

Dr. Hamilton Roe, Physician to the Westminster Hospital, Dr. Hodgkin, Dr. Shaw, Dr. James Johnson, and other eminent medical men, fully corroborate the observations of Sir James Clarke.

It has been seen that, of the amazing quantity of atmospheric air inspired by the lungs, not less than one-eighth of the oxygen which it contains is converted into carbonic acid—a gas highly inimical to animal life. The closeness of the atmosphere in crowded shops which so commonly induces bodily depression, and not unfrequently complete prostration of the physical powers, does not arise from the loss of oxygen alone, but also from the presence of carbonic acid. Animals lowered into the Grotto Del Cane, which cavern or abyss contains this gas in large quantities, become in a few moments completely insensible, and are recovered only by immediate exposure to the air. The melancholy fate of 123 prisoners confined in the Black Hole of Calcutta, 1756, forms a memorable example. Instances in point are of almost daily occurrence. Persons from the same cause frequently faint in crowded and ill-ventilated churches or lecture rooms. The air in such cases is rendered doubly impure ; it not only becomes deprived of its oxygen—the chief supporter of vitality—but charged with an irritating and deleterious gas.

Dr. Combe remarks on this subject as follows :—"On referring to the symptoms induced by breathing carbonic acid gas, or fixed air, it is impossible not to perceive that the head-ache, languor, and debility consequent on confinement in an ill-ventilated apartment, or in air vitiated by many people, are nothing but minor degrees of the same process of poisoning which ensues on immersion in fixed air." Orfila states the chief symptoms of immersion in fixed air, or carbonic acid, to be "great heaviness in the *head, tingling in the ears, troubled sight, a great inclination to sleep, diminution of strength, and falling down.*" "These symptoms," observes Dr. Combe, "as every one knows, closely resemble what is felt in crowded halls."

The Life of Crabbe the Poet, written by his son, contains a profitable illustration. When about ten or eleven years old, Crabbe was sent to a school at Bungay. "Soon after his arrival he had a very narrow escape. He and several of his school-fellows were punished for playing at soldiers, by being put into a large dog-kennel, known by the terrible name of the ' Black Hole.' *George* was the first that entered ; and the place being crammed full with offenders, the atmosphere soon became pestilentially close. The poor boy in vain shrieked that he was about to be suffocated. At last, in despair, he bit the làd next to him violently in the hand. '*Crabbe is dying—Crabbe is dying,*' roared the sufferer ; and the sentinel at length opened the door, and allowed the boys to rush out into the air. My father said, ' a minute more and I must have died.' "

Dr. Jackson, the eminent army surgeon, in urging the necessity of "height of roof as a property of great importance in a house appropriated to the reception of the sick of armies," adds, in support of his views, that "the air being contaminated by the breathing of a crowd of people in a confined space, disease is originated, and mortality is multiplied to an extraordinary extent. It was often proved in the history of the late war, that *more human life was destroyed by accumulating sick men in low and ill-ventilated apartments, than by leaving them exposed, in severe and inclement weather, at the side of a hedge or common dyke.*"—*Sir George Balingal's Lectures,* p. 178.

An anecdote, told of Dr. Adair, is in point A young lady, of gay manners, who visited Bath to place herself under that physician's care, gave a rout, and insisted that the doctor should make one of the party. The company was *numerous*, and the room was *small*. Dr. Adair had not been long at the party, before a young gentleman near to him fell into a *swoon*. The doors and the windows were, of course, immediately thrown open to admit the fresh air. The gentleman who swooned, and the young lady, Dr. Adair's patient, received considerable injury by the sudden exposure to a current of cold air. " How the rest of the company were affected," remarks Dr. Adair, " I had no opportunity of knowing ; but my own feelings and sufferings, for many hours after I retired from this oven, convinced me of the dangerous consequences of such meetings. On declaring a few days after, to one of my brethren, a man of humour, my resolution of writing a bitter philippic against routs, he archly replied, ' Let them alone, Doctor; how could this place otherwise support twenty-six physicians.' "

B. *Peculiar nature of Employments.*—The peculiar nature of employments must regulate our views as to their influence on health. It is usual to characterize the labour of shops as light and easy, and, therefore, not prejudicial to the constitution. Many parents, under this impression, are induced to engage their children, in particular those of weakly constitutions, in such avocations. It is an error, however, fraught with evil consequences. The death of many a tender child, the one fond hope, perhaps, of his still more tender parent, who looks with anxious solicitude to his future career, is attributable to this erroneous system. Deprived of the genial influences of health—exercise and pure air—the lamp of weakly youth, with its already

F

feeble light, yet more and more exhibits symptoms of weakness, until, for want of a due supply of oil, its existence speedily becomes extinguished.

In the minutes of evidence taken before the committee on the Factories' Bill, 1832, a variety of queries in relation to health and the nature of employments, were put to the most eminent physicians and surgeons of this country. The whole of the members of the faculty were agreed, that " employment, ' *light and easy* ' in itself, when continued for such a length of time as to become wearisome both to the mind and to the body, is equally, if not more, prejudicial to the constitution, than more strenuous exertion continued only for a moderate length of time, and with intermissions in the open air." Place the herculean and sturdy ploughman in one of the draper's shops of the metropolis; let him, day after day, and week after week, endure the harassing, though comparatively, 'light and easy' avocations of the counter, and he will soon complain of weariness which he never before experienced, however arduous his labour. His general health too, will quickly display marks of derangement. The constant demands on the mental and physical powers, not irksome in themselves, but almost momently repeated, throughout a great portion of the day, with no appropriate intermissions of rest, even when business is not urgent, produce an irritable state both of mind and body, which is more easily imagined than described. In this light, and thus only, ought the subject to be considered. It will not be difficult to prove that the avocations of the shop are more irksome and depressing than open air employments, which require a much greater amount of bodily exertion. The effects of this system on the physical powers, may be conceived from the weariness or fatigue which individuals experience when in crowded apartments for a length of time. The body soon loses its vigour; an almost complete prostration of the system takes place ; and a few hours suffice to induce a condition of the frame, not experienced even after days of exertion under different and more favourable circumstances.

In reference to the nature of employments and their effects on health, it must not be forgotten, that the condition of the mind has considerable influence on the operations of the body. Labour performed in opposition to the will—when the mind, in fact, is devoid of interest in its performance, produces double the amount of irksomeness and fatigue. It is not uncommon for men to perform extraordinary feats when the mind enters into its performance with freedom or voluntary consent. Compulsory engagements, however, or duties performed for hire, where the will or consent of the mind is not engaged, are limited in their nature, whether it regards duration or degree. The extent of muscular volition, in fact, depends on the condition of the brain. Hence the impolicy of employers who unnecessarily enlarge the duties of their young men. The labour which they obtain is not the fruit of a grateful and cheerful state of the mind, but the effort of a frame uninfluenced by voluntary action.

An assistant draper, whose long experience and respectable character entitles his remarks to careful consideration, after reading the above observations in manuscript, appended the following startling note :—" This point of the question undoubtedly teems with importance. The services of the assistant draper are not the emanation of a cheerful and willing spirit. How can they be so, engaged, as he is, in employment of so monotonous and so harassing a description, and for a period daily which far,—far exceeds the limits of reason and of nature ; and treated moreover by his employer, as in many cases he is, as though he really was composed of different materials? It would indeed be difficult to conceive any class of persons in which so little comparative good feeling exists among the employers and employed, as this class. Excepting those few fortunate ones who have a prospect of commencing business for themselves, these young men, from the yoke which presses upon them, and their consequent utter disgust to the business, are fast using every effort to leave it. Some of them, possessed of a small capital—too small to embark in the drapery business—commence business in the public-house line; others take cigar shops—and some even degrade themselves by becoming the drivers of coaches and omnibuses; anything being, in their opinion, better than an assistant draper. No words can express too strongly the discontent which exists among this class."

The time during which labour can be endured consistent with a due regard to health is a subject of paramount interest. Many important points enter into the consideration of this subject—as the natural powers of the system— age—and, in particular, the peculiar nature of employments. It is seen, with regard to the latter condition, that employments in the open air — involving a more uniform and general exercise of the muscles—with regular meals and appropriate intermissions of rest, are most in accordance with the requirements of health. The *vis naturæ*, or vital power, that self-pre-serving principle of nature which enables man safely to endure ordinary as well as extraordinary physical exertion, depends entirely on the regular and harmonious action of the functions of the system. This pre-supposes a due performance of the organic laws. It demands undeviating attention to the wants of nature It requires appropriate food, air, exercise, and rest, bodily as well as mental. Those employments, which to a greater or less extent withhold these requisites of health, derange and enfeeble the animal functions. The labour of shops, involving as it does—close and long-continued confinement—exposure to an impure atmosphere—want of due exercise—irregular meals—an unnatural prolongation of labour—and interference with the hours of sleep—cannot fail to produce serious and fatal results. Woful experience demonstrates the correctness of these remarks.

How many hours in the day can the human body with safety sustain the exertion of ordinary labour under favourable circumstances? The human frame has been compared, by way of illustration, to a machine of limited powers; one which by previous experiment, is calculated to undergo, for a limited period, a certain degree of labour. If we subject this machine to more labour than it is calculated to perform, in the same proportion will be the limits of its duration. So it is with respect to the human machine. The Creator, in his infinite wisdom, has endowed the constitution of man with vital energy and power sufficient for all natural purposes. The fault of an infringement of nature's laws lies with man and not with God. The intemperate use of the powers of nature debilitates the system, and prema-turely hastens its dissolution. Hence it is, that labour prolonged beyond certain limits, is attended with fatal consequences.

The Greek epigrammatist supposed six hours of daily toil to be the proper portion:

Ἐξ ὡραι μοχθοις ἱκανωταται ἁι δε μετ᾽ ἁντας
Γραμμασι δεικνυεναι ζηθι λεγουσι βροτοις.

Six hours unwearied to stern labour give,
While those that follow cry to mortals " live ! "

The most eminent medical writers of the present day, men of profound knowledge and enlarged experience, concur in opinion that *labour during ten hours each day for a continuance, not including two hours of intermission for meals and recreation, is as much as the human body can sustain with impunity.*

Sir Anthony Carlisle, F.R.S., a Lecturer on Anatomy of great experience, President of the Royal College of Surgeons, remarks, "I am quite satisfied, from my own experience, that is, from forty years of observation and practice in my profession, that vigorous health and the ordinary duration of life cannot be generally maintained under the circumstances of twelve hours' labour, day by day ; *it is incompatible with health, it is not to be done with impunity."*

Dr. James Blundell, Lecturer on Physiology and Midwifery, in the School of Guy's Hospital, London, and an eminent writer in his profession, remarks, "Twelve hours a-day, including two hours for meals, refreshment and rest, are quite sufficient time for human beings to labour for a continuance."

Dr. P. M. Roget, F.R.S., in reference to the question whether "twelve hours a day, with due intermissions for meals, is not ordinarily considered about as much as the human constitution is capable of sustaining with impunity ?" says, "It appears to me that the period mentioned is quite as much as the human frame is calculated to endure for any length of time, even in the adult state." Again—Are not intervals for the taking of meals, during which the labour of the individual shall cease, generally necessary to the preservation of the health of the industrious classes ? I should conceive them quite necessary. Particularly for the recovery of the animal spirits."

Sir William Blizard, F.R.S., Dr. Elliotson, F. R. S., Sir Charles Bell, K.G.H., F.R.S., Sir Benjamin Brodie, F.R.S., Charles Aston Key, Esq., George James Guthrie, F.R.S., Benjamin Travers, Esq., F.R.S., all of them medical writers of eminent talents, and great experience, unite in these views. The same medical gentlemen, also unanimously agree in opinion, that "intervals or cessations from labour, sufficient for taking necessary meals, are essential to health." *Sir A. Carlisle,* when asked whether it was not a received opinion among medical authorities, that "exercise or labour, so long continued as to produce great fatigue, of mind or body, without affording due intermissions for meals, recreation, and sleep, is inconsistent, generally speaking, with the maintenance of health ?" replied, "every one of the points of that question may be answered in the affirmative. I can, from my own experience and knowledge, affirm that it is so."—"This affirmation," continued the same distinguished physician, "is founded upon the principles of my profession, as well as from my own personal experience—and from physiological inductions taken from the whole animal creation, man being part of it, subject to the same laws, or nearly the same laws, as the rest."

Dr. Farre, of London, for forty-two years a consulting physician, goes still further. "I think," he observes, "that twelve hours' labour is too much for a very large majority of human beings. If I am to state the precise quantity, in my experience, as tending to give the longest and most vigorous life, I should take it, even in the adult, at eight hours' active exercise, eight hours' sleep, and eight hours allowed for recreation and meals. Those are the divisions of the day which would procure the happiest and most vigorous life, *and which would, I think, yield the greatest sum of labour.*"

Dr. *Loudon*, one of the medical commissioners appointed in 1833 to collect information in the manufacturing districts, on the employment of children in factories, and the propriety and means of curtailing the hours of labour, remarks, "from fourteen, upwards, I would recommend that no individual should, under any circumstances, work more than twelve hours a-day ; although, if practicable, as a physician, I would prefer the limitation of ten hours, for all persons who earn their bread by their industry." With respect to the above remarks, the second report of the factory commission states, "it should be observed, that they are stated without any exclusive reference to labour in factories, and without any limitation of the age at which the restriction should terminate"—and as it is further observed, "they do not appear more applicable to labour employed in factories than to the mass of other occupations which are followed as a means of subsistence.

The same eminent physicians and surgeons state it as their belief, confirmed by long and extensive experience, that *"the body is in a very unfit state for renewed labour, when the fatigue of the preceding day is not removed by sufficient rest, and when, therefore, the labour has to be resumed in a state of comparative torpor."*

Sir *Wm. Blizard*, F.R.S., upwards of fifty years surgeon to the London Hospital, and upwards of twenty years Lecturer on Surgery and Anatomy to the Royal College of Surgeons, when asked a question of similar import, replied, "Yes ; no doubt, whoever has dwelt upon the intellectual functions, must admit it at once." *Sir Benjamin Brodie, Mr. Guthrie, Mr. Morgan*, surgeon to Guy's Hospital, and Lecturer on Surgery, and others of great eminence in their profession, confirm these important statements.

The value of these testimonies will at once strike the attention of the reader. Unquestionable medical experience demonstrates, that attention to business during twelve hours, deducting two hours intermission for rest and meals, is to the extent as much as the human body can sustain. The labour, however, and confinement of shops and manufactories, often extends to 13, 15, 17, and even longer period, in an atmosphere, and under circumstances peculiarly unfavourable to health. Few young men, of the thousands engaged in shops, rise in the morning with their bodies and minds refreshed by the past night's sleep. The drowsy, care-worn appearance, on the contrary, of a great proportion of this class, exhibits the unhealthy influence of long hours and close confinement. Their capacity for attention to business is of course diminished in exact proportion. Employers, in fact, do not derive any permanent advantage from this unnatural prolongation of labour.

The metropolitan correspondent, from whose interesting communications I have frequent occasion to quote, remarks as follows :—"During that portion of my life, when I was subject to those late hours of business which at present exist in most of the London drapery establishments, so far from being refreshed by my night's sleep, I almost invariably rose from my bed as fatigued and as languid as when I laid down. Of course, this was the result of too great an amount of labour, added to the late hour of my retiring to rest. I believe there are at the present day, thousands who are subject to circumstances of a similarly painful nature. When I look back, I am often at a loss to conceive how I was enabled to go through so many hours of toil, being fatigued at the commencement. Young men are frequently, in some of the later houses, so worn out at night, as to be scarcely able to walk up stairs to their chamber; and innumerable are the instances when, being too exhausted to undress, they have laid themselves down on their beds as they were, and at once falling asleep, have not awoke until morning."

Labour, of whatever description, if it requires one uniform position of the body, proves ultimately injurious.—This observation applies with peculiar force to tailors, dress makers, persons engaged in shops and warehouses, and others of like avocations. Hence, to such individuals, the absolute necessity of an abridgement of the hours of labour. The peculiar *bodily position* of assistants in shops or warehouses, for so long a period, is one of extreme irksomeness, as well as injurious nature, in particular *in early youth, during the period of growth.* A document in the writer's possession, written by one who labours under these evils, speaks of those employed in the drapery establishments of the metropolis and its environs, as continuing at their toilsome duties "from the hours of half-past six and seven in the morning, till those of nine, ten, eleven, and twelve at night, and in many cases till one, two, and sometimes even three o'clock on the following morning, and that during the *whole* of this protracted period of employment, these young persons, whose ages vary principally between the years of 12 and 25, are continually in a *standing* position, with an intermission, at the very extent, of an hour, which includes the time occupied by meals." The consequences are serious in no trifling degree.

Of all natural positions of the body, the erect posture, when long continued, produces most fatigue. Hence, in a recumbent state, the system is said to be at rest. It is in this attitude that man obtains repose. It requires, indeed, extraordinary exertion of the muscular powers to maintain the body for a considerable period, at least, in the erect posture. The muscles have no respite from their labour. The flexure of the spinal column is downwards, and this inclination, combined with the position of the head above, and the bowels in front, forces the body in a forward direction. This tendency is exhibited to a remarkable extent, in attempts to place the dead body in an erect posture, and also in individuals whose muscular powers are weakened by long illness. The weary sensations which all individuals experience, when standing long in much the same position, is proof that certain muscles are unduly exerted. The locomotion induced by employment in shops, is not only limited in extent, but devoid of that character which renders exercise agreeable as well as beneficial. The positions of the body, in attendance upon customers, are often irksome and constrained. They unduly exercise one set of muscles at the expense of others, which are altogether, or for the most part, at rest. Hence, exercise of this kind, independently of the want of pure air, and diversified occupation, is partial and insufficient. It does not develope the physical powers as a whole.

Sir Wm. Blizard remarks, that "the erect position, if long maintained, is unfavourable, in many respects, and leads to consequences very serious," and that labour endured for a considerable length of time, in that posture, "must, of course, render it more distressing to the feelings, and exhausting to the animal frame."

In locomotive exercise, of a diversified kind, the operative muscles have alternate changes of exercise and rest. In the erect position, the same muscles are kept in perpetual action.

The partial exercise of the body in shops, in particular in the standing posture, has an injurious influence on the circulation, whether it respects the nature of the blood, or the due action of the heart. The heart, which has for its office the propulsion of the blood, appropriately to exercise its functions, requires the stimulus of the vital fluid, both as regards quantity and quality. Languid circulation, the natural consequence of confined movements, interferes with this law of nature in both respects. Every other organ of the system, of course, suffers proportionate injury. The evil, however, does not rest here. The brain, duly to perform its office, must be supplied with a certain amount of blood, and the heart performs this office with more labour in the erect posture than in any other.

These, and other considerations, some of which will receive further attention, exhibit the influence of the peculiar nature of employments upon health.

C. *The influence of a dry atmosphere, and unnatural elevation of temperature.*—The functions of the skin exercise an important influence on the animal economy. This delicate and sensitive membrane, is an organ of emoretion, as well as absorption. It is the seat of touch, and also regulates, by means of its excretory office, animal heat. The skin intimately sympathizes with other organs. The bowels, the liver, the lungs, the kidnies, as well as the skin, throw off waste matter. Disorder of each, more or less, exercises an influence on the functions of all. It is in this manner that the unnatural temperature of shops produces numerous otherwise inexplicable disorders of the system.

Relaxation of the skin, by unnatural warmth, tends much to enfeeble its powers of action. The skin, too, to perform its proper functions, must be kept moist.

The rarified state of the atmosphere, produced by the artificial heat of stoves and gas lights, is a fruitful source of ill-health. What young man but recollects the almost insufferable sensations which he experienced when entering upon his new duties? "I well remember," says an assistant draper of the metropolis, in a private communication to the writer, "the night, now just eight years ago, when I first entered on my present sphere of employment. The heat and offensiveness of the gas was so oppressive as scarcely to be borne. It gradually became less susceptible to me, but I fear not on that account much, if any, less injurious. This is the case, more or less, in most shops. In some cases, recourse is had to a species of ventilation, which removes one evil, or partially removes it, at the expense of inflicting another—namely, the influx of a cold current of air, which even in a strong constitution (if there be such a thing in the drapery business) can rarely stand. Cheapness in these matters is generally the first, and as often the principal, consideration."

The high temperature of shops, induces a relaxation of the solids of the system, and expansion of the fluids. The symptoms most manifest are quickened breathing—acceleration of the pulse—fulness and pain in the head, and general bodily uneasiness. Perspiration relieves the latter sensation. This function, indeed, is of two-fold use. It relieves the vessels of their superabundant contents, and the evaporation of the fluid which constantly goes on, not only produces immediate coolness, but deprives the system of its superfluous caloric. In shops, however, where, from the nature of the business, or from an imperfect mode of ventilation, the body is liable to frequent draughts of cold air; this condition is one of extreme danger.

The quickness of breathing, occasioned by an elevation of the temperature in shops, arises from the lungs not receiving the requisite supply of oxygen, and the consequent increased number of inspirations. The contiguity of the heart to the lungs, explains the acceleration of the pulse. The general uneasiness of body is occasioned by the deficiency of pressure, which the absence of moisture, and consequent loss of atmospheric weight, produces.¶ To these symptoms we may add, almost constant thirst. This unpleasant sensation, arises from an unnatural evaporation from the surface of the body, and in particular from the mouth and throat: the consequence of a rarified condition of the air, or diminution of its elastic force.

The warm as well as dry air of those shops which are lighted and warmed by gas and stoves, and consequent evaporation of mucous from the lining membrane of the throat, and air passages, in persons of weak lungs, is not uncommonly accompanied with pain in the chest. The sirocco, that hot and dry air which travellers describe when travelling the sandy deserts of Arabia, produces difficulty of breathing, as well as painful sensations in the chest. The long-continued breathing of hot air, whether from smoking cigars, or exposure to an elevated temperature, combined with the irritation of minute particles of dust, tends, by stimulation, to thicken the delicate membrane of the lungs, and consequently to impair its functions.

Dr. Ure, in an article read before the Royal Society, June, 1836, upon warming and ventilating apartments, relates the result of some most interesting and valuable investigations on the effects of *dry air* on the health. His attention had been drawn to the subject by the Directors of the Customs Fund of Life Assurance, on account of the very general state of indisposition and disease prevailing among those of their officers, (nearly 100 in number) engaged on duty in the long room of the Custom House, London. Dr. Ure describes the symptoms of disorder experienced by several gentlemen (about twenty in number) whom he examined, out of a great number who were indisposed, as very uniform in their character. These were as follows :—" A sense of tension or fullness of the head, with occasional flushings of the countenance, throbbing of the temples, and vertigo, followed, not unfrequently, with a confusion of ideas, very disagreeable to officers occupied with important and sometimes intricate calculations. A few are affected with unpleasant perspiration on their sides. The whole of them complain of a remarkable coldness and languor in their extremities, more especially the legs and feet, which has become habitual, denoting languid circulation in these parts, which requires to be counteracted by the application of warm flannels on going to bed. The pulse is, in many instances, more feeble, frequent, sharp, and irritable, than it ought to be, according to the natural constitution of the individuals. The sensations in the head, occasionally rise to such a height, notwithstanding the most temperate regimen of life, as to require cupping, and at other times depletory remedies. Costiveness, though not a uniform, is yet a prevailing symptom. The sameness of the above ailments, in upwards of one hundred gentlemen, at very various periods of life, and of various temperaments, indicates clearly sameness in the cause."

The temperature of the air in the long room, during the three days of Dr. Ure's experimental inquiry, ranged from 62° to 64° of Fahrenheit's scale. The temperature of the open air on the 7th of January, was 50°, while on the 5th it was only 35°. On both days, however, the thermometer in the long room indicated the same heat, of from 62° to 64°. Dr. Ure observes that the leading characteristic of the air in this room, is its dryness and disagreeable smell. In the long room, the air on the 11th indicated, by Daniel's hygrometer, 70 per cent. of dryness. The external atmosphere was nearly saturated with moisture.—Air, in such a dry state, remarks Dr. Ure, would evaporate 0·44 in. depth of water from a cistern in the course of twenty-four hours; and its influence, he further observes, on the cutaneous exhalents must be proportionably great. "The fetid burned odour of the stove air" remarks the same writer, "and its excessive avidity for moisture, are of themselves sufficient causes of the general indisposition produced among the gentlemen, who are permanently exposed to it in the discharge of their public duties." Dr. Ure thus explains the " permanent action of an artificial desiccated air on the animal economy." "The living body is continually emitting a transpirable matter, the quantity of which, in a grown-up man, will depend partly on the activity of the cutaneous exhalents, and partly on the relative dryness or moisture of the circumambient medium. Its average amount, in common circumstances, has been estimated at 20 ounces in twenty-four hours. When plunged in a very dry air, the insensible perspiration will be increased; and, as it is a true evaporation or gasefaction, it will generate cold proportionably to its amount. Those parts of the body which are most insulated in the air, and furthest from the heart, such as the extremities, will feel this refrigerating influence most powerfully. Hence the coldness of the hands and feet, so generally felt by the inmates of the apartment, though its temperature be at or above 60°. The brain, being screened by the skull from evaporating influence, will remain relatively hot, and will get surcharged, besides, with the fluids which are repelled from the extremities by the condensation, or contraction, of the blood vessels caused by cold. Hence the affections of the head, such as tension, and its dangerous consequences. If sensible perspiration happen, from debility, to break forth from a system previously relaxed, and plunged into dry air, so attractive of vapour, it will be of the kind called a cold clammy sweat on the sides and back, as experienced by many inmates of the long room. *Similar effects have resulted from hot-air stoves, of a similar kind, in many other situations.*" Dr. Ure, from these investigations, agrees with the Directors of the Customs Fund, " that the mode of heating the long room is injurious to the health of persons employed therein, and that it must unduly shorten the duration of life."

The writer considers the above remarks so important and applicable to the subject under consideration, that he has been induced to quote at length from the valuable paper of Dr. Ure. Those who wish to peruse the details in full, can refer to the article " *Stove*" in his Dictionary of Arts and Manufactures.

No effectual artificial means can be employed to remedy the evils under consideration. An artificial temperature, even regulated by the thermometer at the natural point, is highly injurious to health. It lacks the freshening influences which nature effects in the open air. The undulations of the air, in its unconfined condition, remove those impure exhalations from the human system, as well as other atmospheric pollutions, which are the unavoidable concomitants of crowded apartments.

D. *The influence of late hours and long-continued labour during the period of growth.*—The age of a great proportion of those who are engaged in shop avocations, averages from 12 to 25. This period, without doubt, in a

G

physical as well as moral point of view, is the most important in the life of man. The growth of the human body does not usually terminate until 18 or 19 years of age. The powers of life are actively engaged in this process, on the due fulfilment of which depends that natural development, which constitutes health and strength. The structures and functions of the human system, are of an exquisitely delicate description, and require proportionate care to secure the requisite evolution and apportionment of their functions. At this period the functions of circulation and nutrition are in active operation. The gradual augmentation of size and bulk, and consequent building up of the various structures of the body, requires a proportionate supply of nutritious food. In addition to this, the organs of excretion and secretion are unusually active. The supply of food, therefore, must not only be nutritious, but frequent and at proper intervals—proportionate indeed to the rapid powers of digestion. Rapidity of growth, of course, implies a corresponding energy in the circulation of the blood. The nervous system is also in active play, and highly susceptible of external impressions. It is thus that the employments of the boy, exercise a potent and permanent influence on the structure and health of the man. The evil effects of long hours and confinement on young persons, principally depend on the peculiar *position of the body*, and *defective assimilation of material*. Appropriate assimilation requires a due proportion of exercise and pure air. Without these the body quickly droops.

The principal proprietor and sole-acting partner of New Lanark Mills, in reference to the children employed in that manufactory, remarks, "I very soon discovered, that, although these children were extremely well fed, and clothed, and lodged, looked fresh, and, to a superficial observer, healthy in their countenances, yet their limbs were very generally deformed, their growth was stunted, and although one of the best schoolmasters on the old plan was engaged to instruct those children, they made but a very slow progress even in learning the common alphabet."

Sir Astley Cooper thus states the effects of confinement and long hours on the young. It is the conclusion, as he asserts, of extensive observation. "The result of confinement, commonly, is not only to stunt the growth, but to produce deformity, and to that point I can answer, from a good deal of experience, that deformity is a common consequence of considerable confinement." And again, "a person who is full grown certainly suffers from a sedentary mode of life, as well as a child." *Evid. on Manufact.* p, 33, 1816.

Dr. Darwall, in reference to these remarks, observes, "We are the more inclined to confide in this statement, from having made similar observations ourselves in an asylum for children, in a large manufacturing town. Upon an extensive comparison of them with others not so confined, we have no hesitation in saying that their growth was stunted; the buoyancy of infancy, usually so remarkable and engaging, was lost; neither was there that freedom of action in the limbs, which, in children, is generally so conspicuous." These children, he informs us, were properly nourished. Absence of light, want of pure air and appropriate exercise, long continuance in the erect posture, and want of sleep, are the inseparable attendants upon the present system of shop or warehouse business. The consequences upon health are stunted growth, weakness of the muscular powers, deformities of the bones, emaciated frames, and remarkable liability to disease. It would be impossible, in the brief space alloted to this essay, to enumerate the injurious effects of this system on the health of young persons.

Dr. Farre, whose long residence in the West Indies renders him a competent authority, informs us, in relation to the management of the slaves, that "extraordinary care is taken, both in regard to regulating the labour of the young, and in feeding them, to make them a vigorous race and fit for the work." "*I never knew*" says the same physician, "*the young of the negro population over-worked. Their employment was used only as a training for health and future occupation. Even the adult, in the most vigorous condition of body, is not subjected to labour of* 12 *or* 14 *hours duration.*" The slavery, in fact, of our English youth—nay even adults—exceeds in its nature and continuance, the servitude of the negroes in the West Indies.

The statistics of mortality in England, exhibit, to a remarkable extent, the liability of youth to disease during the period of growth. In Paris, the tables of mortality for the year 1820, were as follows:—395 deaths only occurred between the ages of 10 and 15—between the ages of 15 and 20, the mortality increased to no less than 703—or nearly double—in the five years immediately subsequent it rose to 1339—from which period it began to decrease.

Of late years some interesting evidence has been published in reference to the injurious influence of laborious employments on youth, during the period of growth, in particular in connection with the army. Mr. Marshall states, that even in time of peace, when the hardships of a soldier's life are comparatively light, the volunteers received into the army, at the age of 18 or 20, pass two, three, or four years of their period of service (eight years) in the hospital, entirely from their inability to endure exertion, which would produce little or no effect on those who are only a few years more advanced in age.

Sir James Mac. Grigor informs us, that sickness and inefficiency prevailed among our soldiers in Spain, in proportion to the youth and recent arrival of the soldiers. He remarks, that between the 9th of August, 1811, and 20th of May, 1812, the 7th regiment lost 246 men, of whom 169 were recruits, who had landed in the preceding June, and 77 only were old soldiers. The original number of these recruits was 353, *so that more than one-half died within the first eleven months*. The total number of old soldiers was 1143, of whom not more than 77 died during the same period. Sir James Mac. Grigor is convinced, from these and other facts, that "lads are unequal to the harassing duties of the service."

Mr. Marshall informs us, that during the winter of 1805, a French army which was stationed in the neighbourhood of Boulogne, marched about 400 leagues to join the grand army before the battle of Austerlitz, which it effected, "*without leaving almost any sick in the hospitals on the route. The men of this army had served two years, and were not under twenty-two years of age.*" On the other hand, the same writer tells us, that in the campaign of the summer of 1809, "the troops cantoned in the north of Germany, marched to Vienna, but by the time they arrived at the place of their destination, *all the hospitals on the road were filled with sick, more than one-half of the men composing this army were under twenty years of age.*" Napoleon, after the battle of Leipsic, in his efforts to recruit his army, made a call on the legislative senate to render him assistance—"I demand," says he, "a levy of 300,000 men, but *I must have grown men;* BOYS SERVE ONLY TO ENCUMBER THE HOSPITALS AND ROAD-SIDES."

These interesting and conclusive facts show the influence of the undue exercise of the physical powers during the period of youth. It needs no argument to prove that the long hours and close confinement of shops must be no less prejudicial to health and growth. Nay, employment of this nature is in many respects more prejudicial to life. It is true that the exercise which it entails on its victims, is much less arduous in its nature. It is, however, conducted in an impure atmosphere, and under other peculiarly disadvantageous circumstances. Hence it encumbers the hospitals with sick boys to a lamentable extent.

The second Report of the Commissioners on the employment of children, is crowded with examples of the pernicious effects of early labour and long hours on the system during the period of growth. The practice " manifestly interrupts the nutritive functions, and checks the growth of the body," and conjoined with insufficient or unwholesome food, produces "in great numbers of instances, pale, weak and sickly children." *Second Report:* p. 100—560. " The effect of these unfavourable circumstances is greatly to injure the health of the children, and to *stop the growth;* and it is remarkable that the boys are more injured than the girls, because the girls are not put to work as early as the boys, by two years or more. *Ibid.* p. 104—575. In reference to the children employed in the earthenware manufactures, as mould runners, we are told that when not occupied in wedging clay, itself an arduous task, they are incessantly "on the run" from morning till night, always carrying a considerable weight; and the oppressiveness of their labour is, of course, greatly increased by the high temperature in which it is carried on. With scarcely a single exception, the children thus employed are pale, thin, stunted in growth, weak, and unhealthy; most of them suffer from sickness of the stomach, vomiting, and other disorders of the digestive organs. Additional examples of this kind will be adduced in a subsequent division.

The examples of deformity in these districts are almost innumerable. The report of the commissioners literally teems with illustrations. One of the constables of the town of Willenhall says, that " there are examples without number, in the place, of deformed men and boys; their backs or their legs, and often both, grow wrong—the backs grow out and the legs grow in at the knees—hump-backed and knock-kneed." *Ibid.* p.103—572.

E. *The effects of the partial obstruction of light.*—The construction of shops—piled with goods in almost every available space—the street doors, in many instances, so choked with articles, as to have space only for the simple admission of customers—the windows crammed with all the variegated decorations of the season—these circumstances almost entirely exclude one of the most important sources of vigour and health— *the influx of light.* The importance of light, upon animal as well as vegetable life, is a subject of deep interest. Most persons are aware, that the rays of light influence, to a remarkable extent, the colour of flowers. Those flowers which receive due exposure to this influence, display a deepness of tint which is entirely absent when placed under a shade. A plant kept in total darkness, will produce perfectly white flowers. The flowers of the same plant, exposed to the influence of light, will exhibit the brilliant and variegated hues of nature. The absence of light produces analogous effects on animals. Light exercises an important influence on growth. Dr.

Edwards, the celebrated physiologist, ascertained by experiment that tadpoles, when excluded from light, continue to grow, but never become frogs. Dr. Edwards attributes the absence of deformity among the Caribs, Mexicans, Peruvians, and other uncivilized nations, to their continual exposure to the light. He supposes, also, that much of the sickness which prevails in prisons, as well as a considerable proportion of the scrofula which afflicts those children who reside in confined situations, arises from the absence of light. All physiologists admit that light is a most salutary agent in promoting the due development of young animals. It increases the tension and solidity of the muscular fibres, and, consequently, acts as a stimulant, or tonic. The absence of light relaxes the skin ; and, hence, persons in the shade are more liable to perspiration. Hence, also, it is, that even in tropical climates, men exposed to the action of light are active and vigorous, while persons residing in confined apartments are indolent, and unable to endure fatigue. Persons, therefore, so long confined in shops as at present constructed, are, to a considerable extent, deprived of one of those natural influences which are essential to health.

F. *The effects of late hours in business on the ,eyes.*—The second report of the commissioners contains numerous illustrations of the injurious influence of long-continued labour on the delicate organs of the sight.

In the glass-trade, we are told, that the young hands who "are generally pale, thin, ill-grown, and unhealthy," suffer "severely from bad eyes." The "eyes of many are bloodshot ; 'nearly blind for weeks together ;' 'he constantly had sore eyes since he was at this glass house.'" These, and other similar remarks, are of frequent occurrence.

In reference to the children who work at machine lace, it is stated that "their health and sight are often greatly impaired, especially among the runners, who occasionally faint whilst at work ;" again, "short-sightedness, amaurosis, distortion of the spine, excessive constitutional debility, indigestion, and derangement of the uterine functions, may be said *to be almost universal.*" "There cannot be," remark the commissioners, "an occupation which more seriously deteriorates the constitution."—*Second Report*, p. 111—607.

In the hosiery trade, the strain upon the eyes causes "the sight to be seriously injured." "Spectacles are commonly required at forty." Of the poor children employed as cheveners, it is said that they become so near-sighted as not to be able to see the clock across the room.—*Ibid*. p. 111—608.

The medical witnesses examined in reference to the condition of the poor dress makers inform us, that "all forms of ocular disease are induced, from simple irritation to complete blindness," by the system of late hours and protracted labour, common to that unfortunate class.

G. *The influence of the system, in a dietetic point of view.*—Health mainly depends on the proper performance of the functions of digestion. A disordered condition of the stomach, more or less, influences all the functions of the human frame.

> It is the storehouse and the shop of
> The whole body. True it is,
> That it receives the general food at first,
> But all the cranks and offices of man,
> The strongest nerves, and small inferior veins,
> From it receive that natural competence
> Whereby they live.   SHAKSPERE.

Trade, as at present conducted, prevents due attention to those laws on which depends the proper performance of the functions of digestion. This remark particularly applies to assistants and warehousemen. "Dinner rarely occupies," says an experienced assistant, "more than fifteen, and each other meal only ten minutes. The moment they have *bolted* their food, they are expected to return to business." The influence of this practice on health will now receive brief consideration. Man cannot with impunity infringe the laws of Omnipotence.

The time devoted to meals is of great importance.—Hurried repasts involve unavoidable neglect of several duties. Slow and perfect mastication is absolutely essential to health. Nature provides three sets of glands to secrete that important fluid called the saliva. This secretion is obviously designed to be mixed with the food during the act of mastication. Hurried meals, of course, defeat this object, and, consequently, impair digestion. *Perfect mastication*, which, of course, implies *slow eating*, is necessary to ascertain the bounds of lawful appetite. The appetite, in quick eaters, often continues after the stomach has received a greater amount of food than it can well digest. Hence one prolific source of indigestion.

"Quick at meat, quick at work," is a maxim too much in vogue among tradesmen. It is pregnant with numerous evils. The Arabs have a proverb to the effect that " he who does not take care to chew his victuals hates his life." The Germans, also, have an adage, that "food well masticated is half digested." There is much force in these apophthegms, as experience testifies. Indigestion is a source of numerous ailments. It produces a long train of nervous and hypochondriacal feelings, which often unfit the mind for attention to business—at least in that spirit which renders it pleasant as well as profitable. Hence, employers, in abridging the time for meals, act against their own interests.

The gastric juice, a fluid secreted from the coats of the stomach, effects important and essential changes on the food. *This secretion always bears a direct relation to the quantity of aliment naturally required by the system.* If, therefore, for want of due attention to the bounds of appetite, which the hurried meals of persons engaged in shops does not admit, food is swallowed in greater proportion than nature requires, it becomes a painful source of irritation and annoyance. The undigested food, that portion, in fact, for which there is not a sufficient amount of gastric juice to dissolve, becomes subject to chemical laws. Hence, an additional prolific source of indigestion.

Persons of weak and dyspeptic habits, in particular, should never sit down to meals in a state of fatigue. The depressed condition of the vital powers, under such circumstances, acts unfavourably on digestion. An experiment in point is on record. Two hounds were fed with their usual food, and under similar circumstances. The one was left to sleep, while the other was immediately led to the chase. On the return of the latter, both animals were killed. The food in the stomach of the dog which had slept, was nearly digested. In the other animal, it remained entirely unaltered.

Too much exercise, either of mind or body, impedes digestion. It is on this account that diseases of the digestive organs much prevail among shopmen, and persons of literary habits. They do not allow time for the stomach to convert the food into chyme. The consent of the mind, indeed, is essential to perfect digestion. The mind and body, harassed

a long series of vibrations, and demand bracing up." The correctness and force of the remarks will be recognized by thousands, who toil day after day in our shops under the present circumstances of trade.

b. Appearance and complexion.—Sallowness of complexion arises from several causes. A torpid condition of the liver, however, and consequent imperfect elimination of the biliary secretion from the blood, is the main source of this unhealthy appearance. The bile remains mixed with the blood, and tinges the surface of the body by means of the circulation. The frequent collapse occasioned by unequal exposure, from the high temperature of shops, to the low temperature of the external air, in particular at night, and the consequent effects on the circulation, is a frequent cause of that torpid state of the liver, which disqualifies that important organ from the due performance of its functions.

Sallowness of the skin is indicative, either of functional organic disturbance of the organs of digestion, or a want of energy in the circulation. The absence of light, so common in the great proportion of drapers' shops, is one cause of the unhealthy complexion of young men. It is easy to distinguish a shop youth by his complexion.

c. Muscular power and weight—stature—thinness.—The result of parliamentary investigation, some years ago, was to demonstrate, that "those engaged in mills and factories, weigh considerably lighter than others engaged in different pursuits, such as are ordinarily followed in the open air, and under more favourable circumstances." It was also ascertained, "on very careful examination, that the stature of the children so employed, compared with the height of others differently occupied, is considerably less." These remarks apply with equal force to the young men employed in shops. It would, indeed, be difficult to find one assistant draper exhibiting that muscular development, or ordinary stature of individuals engaged in athletic and open door exercise. One of their own body remarks, in a communication to the writer, "as a proof of the unhealthy tendency of the present system—it is only necessary to look at young men so employed—out of so numerous a class there is scarcely an individual who deserves the name of man."

The general condition of the children employed in the manufacturing districts, demonstrates the truth of the above remarks : Pin-headers have often the appearance of being stunted in their growth ; the generality of them are short and weakly." *Second Report of Commiss.* p. 100—562. One of the examining surgeons, for the recruiting service in Birmingham states, "the mechanics are shorter, more puny, and altogether inferior in their physical powers ; many of the men are distorted in the spine and chest." One sergeant says, " the mechanics are generally shorter than in any other town he has known, the general height being from five feet four inches, to five feet five inches." *Ibid.* Out of 613 men enlisted, almost all of whom came from Birmingham, and five other neighbouring towns, only 238 were approved for service. *Ibid.*

In Wolverhampton, the children were so stunted, that the sub-commissioner, "during his first examinations, was unable to credit the statement they made of their ages," and " with very few exceptions they were all alike." *Ibid.* p. 103—569. The expressions used by the sub-commissioner, in numerous instances, are " a very poor weakly-looking creature," " utterly stunted and deformed," " growth utterly stunted," " very poorly grown, stunted, wretchedly thin."

H

The remarkable thinness, as well as paleness, of drapers and other assistants, demonstrates the unhealthy nature of their employment. The paleness, of course, indicates the want of pure air and healthy circulation of the blood. The peculiar thinness of the body arises from an imperfect performance of lacteal absorption, in other words, the absorption of nutriment from the alimentary canal. If the body cannot obtain its due supply of nutriment from other sources, *it will live on itself.* In over-labour the balance between lacteal and lymphatic absorption is disturbed, and the latter class of vessels first take up the fluids, and then the solids of the system. Thus a diminution of the muscular fibre, and consequent power or capacity, and even to some extent the earthy structure of the bones themselves.

d. Disorder of the stomach and bowels.—The habits of shopmen, in reference to diet, explain the almost universal prevalence of indigestion among this class. So imperfect, indeed, are their powers of digestion, that it is rare to find a clean tongue among individuals thus employed. Nor is this circumstance at all calculated to excite surprise. It is the result of involuntary neglect of the laws of health.

The lungs suffer materially from imperfect digestion of the food. Hence, the prevalence of " dyspeptic pthisis," or "consumption from bad digestion," among those persons who are confined to shops during so long a period. Dr. Combe attributes these evils to "late hours, heavy meals, and deficient exercise."

Mr. Thackrah, in his able work on the Effects of Arts, Trades and Professions on health, states, that dyspeptic symptoms often first indicate the commencement of disease. The lungs, he remarks, only exhibit signs of mischief some time after disorders of the digestive functions.

A torpid state of the bowels is an almost invariable consequence of these habits. The action of the bowels depends chiefly on the vigour of the muscular fibres, and a due secretion of mucus from its lining membrane. The habits of shopmen interfere with both, and hence, the universal prevalence of constipation, with its thousand evils.

An assistant draper writes as follows:—" I suffered greatly from constipation for a considerable period. So much so, that I believe I may state, without the least deviation from truth, that for 3 or 4 years after my first 12 months residence in London, I scarcely experienced one single natural action of the bowels. During that period I had abundance of in-door wearisome employment, but no exercise, or next to none, in the open air. I had constant recourse to medicines without deriving any other advantage than a temporary one—and to have talked to one, who from the lateness of business, rarely saw his chamber during the summer season until twelve, one, or two o'clock at night—about rising sufficiently early to take outdoor exercise, would have been worse than useless—it would, in fact, have been mere mockery. Having recently, however, been more favourably situated in regard to the period of my employment, I have been privileged to retire to bed at a reasonable hour, and without suffering so much fatigue, by which I have been enabled to rise up sufficiently early to take a walk, or have recourse to other out-door muscular exercise, previously to the commencement of my usual duties. I am now, thank God, in the enjoyment of tolerably good health. So far from it being absolutely necessary, as I have stated was previously the case, that I should have recourse to medicine at least once a *week*, it is now nearly *six months* since I have taken a single dose. I do not require it."

e. Affections of the lungs and air pipes.—The writer has often witnessed with indescribable pain, the injurious, nay—it is not too harsh language to characterize it as—murderous, effects of long hours and close confinement, in particular on youths from agricultural districts. Their appearance, on first entrance into business, is, in general, indicative of robust health—their movements are characteristic of the elasticity and buoyancy of youth, not diminished, as we may readily suppose, by the novelty and stirring nature of new and exciting scenes. Late hours and close confinement, soon, alas, suffice to effect melancholy changes. The glow of health speedily gives place to the pale hue and sunken cheek ; the countenance quickly assumes a fretful and care-worn aspect; the lagging and imperfect movements of the body exhibit the changes in the physical man, that are slowly, but effectively, working within ; the hectic flush and the hollow cough next make their appearance, and consumption, that fell disease of English youth terminates the distressing scene. This picture is neither too highly wrought, nor drawn from imagination, but the heart-rending result of the writers professional experience.

Consumption prevails, to a fearful extent, among dress-makers and milliners. Mr. Devonald, surgeon, who had witnessed the health of several who had married, and whom he had attended for years, says, "their health and strength are gone ; they are completely disorganised ; has known numbers of healthy young women, who in this way have been reduced to a permanent state of debility. Many of them die, especially from consumption." *Grainger, Evidence :* p. *f.* 236, ll. 16. 20.

Inflammation of the bronchial tubes, or air pipes, is of common occurrence among individuals engaged in sedentary occupations. It too often happens that young men, wearied almost to faintness with the labours of the day, and unable to resist the temptation of a stroll after the hours of business, either thoughtlessly expose their lungs to the humid and chilly air of the night, or with the delusive notion of counteracting the bad effects of exposure at so late an hour, indulge in the pernicious and fatal practice of smoking cigars. Both these habits sow the seeds of incurable disease. The condensation at night, of that moisture which has been absorbed from the earth during the day, renders an exposure at this period, in no trifling degree, prejudicial to the health of those who are confined for a considerable period in an elevated temperature. In addition to the noxious state of the atmosphere at night, bodies excited during the day with unnatural heat, are exposed to the depressing influence of a low temperature. The skin, in fact, all the powers of the system, are in a favourable condition to unhealthy impressions. Hence, the origin of fatal disease, in particular in the lungs.

f. Mortality produced by the system.—The general effects of late hours in business, combined with undue exertion of the animal powers, are, 1. *A tendency to disease.* 2. *A diminished power of resisting disease ;* and 3. *A greater fatality of disease.*—The physical man is slowly, but effectively undermined by a multitude of causes, in themselves and considered apart, not calculated to excite alarm, but, when combined, producing a serious condition of the system. Thus, on the attack of disease, that vital power on which recovery from serious illness mainly depends, is at a low ebb, and disorders which, under ordinary circumstances, would soon yield to simple remedial treatment, are either protracted in their duration, or rapidly terminate in death. The writer can call to recollection numerous melancholy illustrations.

Mr. Thackrah speaks of "the circumstances of civic life, which for years, inflict no perceptible injury, [but] may, and probably do, shorten the duration of life." " In other words," he continues, " health is often preserved at the expense of that vital power, which, in a more natural state, would have carried us to an age." Dr. Combe observes, "many circumstances rarely considered as injurious, because they have no immediate effect in suddenly destroying life by acute disease, have, nevertheless, a marked influence in slowly undermining health and shortening human existence. There are trades, for example, at which workmen may labour for fifteen or twenty years, without having been a month confined by disease during all that time, and which are therefore said to be healthy trades ; and yet, when the investigation is pursued a little farther, it is found that the general health is so steadily, although imperceptibly, encroached upon, that scarcely a single workman survives his fortieth or fiftieth year."

The statistics on mortality decisively corroborate these views. The mortality in towns whose inhabitants reside in a comparatively impure atmosphere, and labour in confined apartments for an unnatural length of time, is much greater than in agricultural districts. At birth, the probability of life is averaged at 25 years. In the North Riding of Yorkshire, an agricultural district, one half that are born live to 30 years. In the West Riding, however, or manufacturing district of the same county, not less than half die before they arrive at the age of 18. In Lancashire and the cotton districts half do not live to 12 years of age. The mean duration of life in the towns and rural situations differs, according to Mr. Farr, the registrar-general, by nearly 17 years. The average of life, according to the last census, being 55 years in the country, and only 38 in the towns.

London occupies in space about 20 square miles. In 1835, its population was 1,776,600. This population exceeds considerably that of the four great western counties, Somerset, Dorset, Devon, and Cornwall, whose area is not less than 6,553 miles, and population in 1831, 1,358,868. The difference in mortality need not, after these details, excite surprise. Dr. Hogg informs us, that not only does animal life suffer in London from an impure atmosphere, but also that the trees, shrubs, and plants that are nursed in the squares and conservatories, dwindle and die in frequent succession, and evidently from want of the vivifying influence of pure air.

Mr. Thackrah remarks, that life in some is worn out by excess in labour : more frequently, he continues, it is reduced and shortened by the want of its natural food—an atmosphere pure and free. Persons engaged in baneful occupations, as masons, live on the average 10 years longer in the country than in the town. In examining factories, exclaims the same gentleman, we have frequently asked, " Where are the *old* men ?" Our towns and manufactures present but a small proportion. The same question may be put with respect to our shopkeepers and their assistants,— " Where are the *old* men ?" and, alas, the answer will present a fearful blank.

IV. *Incidental evils.*—These are various, and will be discussed under separate heads.

A. *Interference of Saturday evening-trading with the duties of the Sabbath.*—The sanctification of the Sabbath implies rest from all worldly transactions. " To discharge oneself from worldly employments, for the service of God and religion," is the brief but expressive command of the Alamannic laws. To be properly observed, the Sabbath must be *commenced* in a suitable spirit. The present mode of conducting business on Saturday nights, often renders the fulfilment of this duty difficult, if not impracticable. Most retail shops are kept open until the clock strikes twelve, and afterwards half an hour, an hour, or even in some shops, longer space of time is occupied on the Lord's Day, in siding goods, sweeping floors, rubbing counters, and other unseemly and incongruous acts. This practice, surely will be admitted, by all Christians, to be an unnecessary and unjustifiable desecration of the day appointed for the worship of the Most High.

It is notorious that the duties of assistants are much more laborious and exhausting on Saturday than on any other day in the week. On this day sixteen hours are usually devoted to incessant application. Is it not unreasonable, that this period, of all others in the week, should be devoted to extraordinary labour—labour which often unfits the mind for its sacred duties on the following day? Hence, the weary state of body and mental listlessness which youths employed in shops, exhibit on the Sabbath.

The extraordinary late business hours of Saturday nights, by their interference with early rising, render it impracticable for a great portion of our young men to engage in Sabbath instruction. An entire change in the system would enable numbers of our youth to impart to others, yet more humble in the scale of society, those stores of knowledge, which an abridgement of the hours of labour would enable them to acquire.

In the Sunday school connected with the church of which the writer's esteemed friend, the Rev. Hugh Stowell, is incumbent, out of 100 teachers, only five are occupied during the week in shop employments. In Bennett Street school, Manchester, there are not less than from one to two hundred teachers engaged in Sabbath instruction; of these not more than six are similarly employed during the week.

" I am intimately acquainted," remarks a metropolitan assistant draper, " with a young man, who has been accustomed, for several years, to teach in a sabbath school. I was present when his medical adviser told him, that he must give up his usual Sunday avocations, in order to obtain that of which, on business days, he was deprived—namely, exercise in the open air. Now, was business suspended, as it should be, at 7 or 8 o'clock in the evening—relieved from the weariness of their employment—not driven, as at present, by feelings bordering closely upon exhaustion, for stimulants to a neighbouring tavern—with some judicious plan for their improvement, there are the strongest reasons for hoping that thousands, now wallowing in the mire of sensuality, would, ere long, be induced to give up their evil ways, and attend to those things which alone are worthy the attention of beings destined for immortality; and my friend also, with a large number of others, similarly situated, possessing opportunity to obtain a due supply of fresh air and relaxation during the week, would, on the Sabbath, be enabled to resume, without injury, his usual and favourite employment. Thus, doubtless, many valuable lives would be preserved, the amount of human health augmented, that of immorality lessened, and true religion promoted."

To abridge *God's* portion of our time, merely to lengthen *our own*, is a crime of no mean magnitude. It is robbery of the Most High. Nor is the offence less culpable in its nature, that we devote the time thus sacrilegiously obtained to the selfishness of gain.

Ancient nations, whether sacred or profane, held it an inviolable duty not to interfere with the time appointed for devotional purposes. The *Feriæ*, or sacred days of the Romans, long before the introduction of christian principles, rigidly began and ended at midnight. In this respect the heathens of antiquity set us an example worthy of imitation. The christians of past ages were so anxious to *commence* the sabbath in a proper spirit that laws were specially enacted for this purpose. Among the Franks, King Childebert the First, A. D. 555, inflicted severe penalties on those who spent either the *vigils*, or the evenings themselves of days devoted to religion, such as Christmas and Easter, in an irregular manner. He particularly specifies indulgence in excesses on Saturday evenings, which he characterizes as no less than sacrilege and an indignity offered to God. The English Saxons, our remote ancestors, were rigidly attentive to this point. The constitution of Withred, King of Kent, and of the council of Berghamsted, A. D. 697, defined the limits of the sabbath to be from sunset on Saturday evening to Sunday night. King Edgar, in his Ecclesiastical laws, A. D. 967, extended yet further the limits of the Lord's day, that is, *from three o'clock on Saturday afternoon to the break of day on Monday*. The law of Canute, on this subject, was expressed almost in the same words. Edward the Confessor, directed that the sabbath should extend to the same period. This was one of those enactments which were afterwards confirmed by William the Norman. Withred, King of Kent, ordained that if a servant did any servile work, by order of his master, any time from sunset on Saturday till after sunset on the Lord's day, the latter was to be fined the sum of eighty shillings.

These examples of bygone enactments exhibit the scrupulous regard which our remote ancestors had for the due observance of the sabbath. No worldly business, of whatever description, was transacted on any part of this day of rest, nor were the hours immediately preceding its specific limits to be engaged in pursuits, which would disturb that calm and peaceful state of mind which is alone calculated to render its observance spiritual and profitable.

In the preceding pages, numerous instances are mentioned of sabbath profanation in connection with business—in particular in relation to dress makers and milliners. The limits of this essay forbid the further extension of this subject, or many pages might be filled with similar details.

B. *Its interference with domestic and social intercourse, family worship, and other duties.*—The system of late hours in business interferes with the social and domestic duties and enjoyments, whether of employers or their young men. Man is a social being. The interchanges and associations of friendship, and, above all, the endearing relations of domestic intercourse, are well calculated, under the guidance of religion, to soothe the sorrows, and to mitigate the asperities of life. The nature of man requires those bonds of affectionate sympathy and reciprocal interchange which domestic enjoyments alone afford.

> *Domestic happiness, thou only bliss*
> *Of Paradise, that has survived the fall!*
> *Though few now taste thee unimpaired and pure,*
> *Or tasting, long enjoy thee! too infirm,*
> *Or too incautious, to preserve thy sweets*
> *Unmixed with drops of bitter, which neglect*
> *Or temper sheds into thy crystal cup:*
> *Thou art the nurse of virtue; in thine arms*
> *She smiles, appearing, as in truth she is,*
> *Heaven-born, and destined to the skies again.*
> *Thou art not known where pleasure is adored.*

is comparatively trifling. It is the monotonous and continued daily exposure to a noxious atmosphere, rendered trebly injurious by the combined influence of night air, a temperature, either rendered hot by the season, or the effects of gas, and respiration in an atmosphere necessarily rendered impure by the numerous customers of large shops. It must not be forgotten, that the excitement of continued attention to, and conversation with a constant stream of visitors, under these circumstances, increases the action of the lungs, so that unfortunately for the health of our young men, respiration is most active at a period, when the air which they breathe is deleterious to an unusual degree. Increased respiration of course implies a corresponding increase in the supply. If for example the supply, calculating 80 pulses in the minute, be two gallons of air, the demand when the pulse is raised to 100 per minute, will be one-fifth more. These facts require serious consideration.

The same remarks apply with equal, indeed much greater force, to the vast number of children of both sexes, often confined during the whole night at their arduous avocations. It is a system fraught with evil consequences.

D. Its prevention of the practice of early rising.—Early rising is as essential to the maintenance of health, as early rest. This habit is in the highest degree conducive to long life. In no point, indeed, is there such unanimous accordance in practice among long-lived individuals. The old adage, " early to bed and early to rise" is familiar to all, and early rising of course implies, retiring to rest at an appropriate early hour in the evening. The system of late hours, however, in the transaction of business, renders it impossible for thousands of our young men to adopt a plan, which would in many respects advantage their health. Many of our most eminent writers, whether of ancient or modern times, attribute their vigorous health and extraordinary mental efforts to the practice of early rising. Among other illustrious examples, we may mention Alfred of England, Sir Thomas More, Linnæus, Bishop's Burnet, Horne, and Jewell, Drs. Tissot, Paley, Kippis, Franklin, Priestley, Parkhurst, Doddridge, Sir Walter Scott, Mr. Wesley, Buffon, and a host of others distinguished for their intellectual labours. If our young men were enabled, by an alteration in business hours, to retire early to rest, it would be in their power, during the summer months at least, to enjoy a morning's ramble,—a practice which would contribute to their health, and obviate to a considerable extent the injurious consequences of close confinement during the day. " Many," remarks a late judicious writer, " of the immense number of persons who procure their livelihood in sedentary occupations, in the metropolis and other large cities, and are, consequently, obliged to reside there, conceive that, as they must of necessity submit to their lot in life, it is useless to give themselves any concern to counteract the evils attendant upon it. For many years, I have myself resided in London, and have been occupied in sedentary employments, but being convinced that inactivity and perpetually respiring a confined and vitiated air must be prejudicial to health, I resolved to pass as many hours as I could spare in exercise in a pure atmosphere : for this purpose, I rose early in the morning, and either walked or rode as far into the country as my time would permit, and repeated the same exercise after I had concluded the avocations of the day. This practice I regularly pursued, without interruption, and soon found I obtained in this manner, as sound and uninterrupted health, as is enjoyed by those residing wholly in the

I

country." It has been observed, with considerable truth, that the man who neglects the beauties of the early morning hour, but half enjoys his existence. The author of the "Seasons" has the following exquisite lines on this subject :

> Falsely luxurious, will not man awake,
> And springing from the bed of sloth, enjoy
> The cool, the fragrant, and the silent hour,
> To meditation due and sacred song?
> For is there ought in sleep can charm the wise?
> To lie in dead oblivion: losing half
> The fleeting moments of too short a life;
> Total extinction of the enlightened soul!
> Or else, to feverish vanity alive
> Wildered, and tossing through distempered dreams?
> Who would in such a gloomy state remain
> Longer than nature craves, when every muse,
> And every blooming pleasure wait without
> To bless the wildly devious morning walk.

The statements and facts advanced in this division of the essay, present but to a limited extent, the moral and physical evils which the system of late hours in business entails on its unfortunate victims. The poet well exclaims,

> "Man's inhumanity to man
> Makes countless thousands mourn."

Eternity alone will unfold the dreadful reality.

DIVISION THE FOURTH.

MOTIVES FOR AN ALTERATION IN THE SYSTEM.

The preceding pages of this essay have been occupied, briefly and imperfectly it is true, in an exposure of some of those evils which either directly arise from, or are intimately associated with, the system of late hours in trading. If the statements made be correct, and the writer has, in every instance, carefully appealed either to unquestionable authorities, or to the result of his own wide and extensive professional experience, it must be evident to all who reflect seriously on the subject, that national, as well as individual interests, loudly call for an alteration in a state of things, no less opposed to the designs of the Creator, as displayed in the constitution of man, than to the general tenor of the Scriptures.

I. *In reference to the employed.*—An abridgement in the hours of labour would be an advantage to young men, because

1st. It would enable them to obtain the benefits of *pure air, exercise, change of scene, and innocent and rational recreation,* privileges which would, to a considerable extent, counteract the effects of close confinement and anxious and monotonous duties ; and

2ndly. It would afford them time for intellectual and moral elevation, and consequently enable them to improve their condition in life.

Individuals engaged in laborious occupations during the day, would obtain the rest necessary to restore the functions of exhausted nature, while on the other hand, those whose employments are sedentary, would have that exercise within their reach which is essential to the maintenance of uninterrupted health. Long-continued and close confinement in our retail shops, ruins the health of our young men, destroys their social and domestic comfort—prevents them from acquiring useful information, and induces them to form habits, which not only degrade them in the scale of society, but obstruct their successful career in life.

It is useless to expect healthful morals in young men while exposed to the influence of this pernicious system. Deprived of reasonable opportunities of relaxation, they resort in the brief intervals at their disposal to secret but vitiated enjoyments—croud days into moments—rush heedless, in fact, into those seductive enjoyments which ensnare thousands of our unguarded youth.

The fear that young men would make an improper use of the privilege, is an objection made by some to the proposed change.—This objection would appear to be rather general, if the writer must judge from the tenor of several letters which he has received from distinguished individuals on the subject. One talented and benevolent correspondent writes—" In respect to the morals of young men, more liberty more mischief," and quotes the lines—" Satan finds some mischief still, for idle hands to do." The remark, in its original sense, is correct and forcible. It is unjust, however, to presume, that if young men had their evenings to themselves, they would necessarily be *idle*, or run, as anticipated, into all kinds of excess. This plan, *even if true*, is no sufficient reason for the continuance of the practice. The mere supposition, for it has no claim to a stronger appellation, that young men may act unjustly towards themselves, is no palliation of the injustice of the system towards young men. It is irrational and absurd, moreover, to urge the abuse of liberty as a reason why we should withhold its exercise. Besides, if the conduct of young men in the first instance, should not in all respects be as consistent and correct as might be desired, are we not justified in attributing the consequences to the system itself, as its natural and unavoidable fruits. In other words, ought we not to trace the *effects* to their proper and legitimate *cause?*

The following remarks of Dr. Combe are forcible and to the point :— " After excessive employment in an impure atmosphere, languor, debility, and exhaustion necessarily follow, and the individual is left susceptible of no stimulus but that of ardent spirit, or of excited and reckless passion."

It is manifest that the system has had an injurious influence on the character and welfare of a numerous portion of our youth. It is no less evident that it does not owe its origin or continuance to the young men themselves. On the contrary, they are the victims of a practice over which, as a body, they have no control. The representatives of a numerous and most respectable, and influential class of assistants in the metropolis, in an address recently issued, remark, " *there can be do doubt in the mind of those best informed on the subject, that the present late-hour system is the most fertile source of the immorality which prevails amongst us, and which, whilst we are bound to acknowledge its existence, it is our sincere desire to counteract.*" This extract is from a late address of the central committee of Metropolitan assistant drapers. Here then, in connection with an anxious appeal for assistance, is a candid and honourable acknowledgement of the existence of evils, which whether it regards individual or national interests, it is most desirable to remove—an appeal and acknowledgement too, issued by the very class of individuals amongst whom the evils exist. And to whom may they confidently and justly look for active assistance, but to those employers, and that portion of the public, whose unreasonable demands upon their time and exertions, is the direct source of the grievous and intolerable evils under which they labour. And shall this appeal—honourable as it is to the heads and hearts of those from whom it has issued, be permitted to pass in unmerited silence and neglect? Let the Christians of enlightened England decide. The young men of the Metropolis, and our large towns; in their application for an abridgement of the hours of labour, seek the concession of just and equitable claims. They only solicit those reasonable opportunities of improvement, whether it relates to their moral, physical, or intellectual condition, which every man by his birthright ought to possess, the proper fulfilment of which, be it remembered, God demands at their hands. Gross deficiencies in these points, may, without injustice, be charged upon those who support, and consequently perpetuate, a system as unjust as it is injurious. Let not imaginary fears obstruct the concession of these equitable demands. If our conscience assures us that the concession sought is founded in equity and justice, let us do our duty, and leave the consequences to the disposal of Omnipotence.

The time required for the production of the necessaries and conveniences of life, has of late years been much lessened by the aid of machinery. A moderate expenditure of labour is now only required for this purpose. The *lot* of the labourer, however, seems rather increased than diminished by the results of invention. " It appears to me," says Dr. Dick, " that the Governor of the world, in permitting such inventions for facilitating the process of manufactures, evidently intends thereby, that the period of human labour should be abridged, in order to afford scope to all classes of society for mental, moral, and religious improvement; in order to prepare the way for that period, when the knowledge of the Lord shall cover the earth, it ought, therefore, to be considered as a misapplication of machinery, when it is employed chiefly for the purpose of enriching and aggrandizing a few individuals, while the mechanic and labourer are deprived both of the physical and moral advantages which it was intended to produce." It is thus that sinful men ever frustrate the benevolence of the Deity.

II. *In reference to employers.*—An abridgement of the hours of labour would benefit employers, because, 1. It would enable manufacturers to produce goods of a better quality, devoid of those frequent blemishes which characterize articles produced by prolonged or night labour.—2. It would elevate the character and intelligence, and consequent value of their young men, by affording them reasonable opportunities for instruction.—3. It would reduce, in various ways, their expenditure, while it would not in the least diminish their lawful gains.—4. It would enable them to afford higher and more equitable remuneration to those in their employ, and to some extent at least to reduce the price of goods.—5. It would enable them to enjoy the pleasures of domestic intercourse—to superintend the education and morals of their children—to devote a portion of their time to intellectual cultivation, as well as recreation, and to attend to the duties of domestic worship.

Increased intelligence among our young men, superinduced on improved habits, would render them of much greater value to their employers.—It needs little argument to show, that an increase in intelligence and morals, would render assistants and clerks not only more effective in their duties, but better entitled to offices of trust and confidence. It is of great importance that young men engaged in duties of this nature, should be methodical and correct in their books. Errors in accounts operate most injuriously on the interests of employers. On the one hand, a deficiency in the account deprives employers of their just demands; on the other, an overcharge made to purchasers, and in particular if repeated, excites suspicions in the minds of the latter prejudicial to the tradesman's interests, and even otherwise, inconveniences are occasioned, which commonly result in the loss of custom. Intelligent and well-principled young men will be just in their dealings to all parties—just to their employers—just to those who purchase. They will dedicate their whole time to the interests of those in whose service they are engaged. The attention which they will devote to business, will not be that of eye-service alone—no apparent devotion of attention during the presence of their employers, and carelessness and frivolity in their absence—but a uniformly constant attention from principle —attention which will evince an anxious desire to promote their master's interest, even as if it were their own.

The value of labour does not so much depend on its duration, as on its energy and effectiveness.—The mistaken policy of employers, in reference to this subject, has led to no trifling deprivation on the part of young men engaged as clerks or assistants. The human machine is endowed with limited powers ; and undue exercise, whether of mind or body, tends to exhaust its energies and to diminish its capabilities of duration. It is useless to expect long-continued satisfactory exertion from individuals whose frames are prostrated by labour disproportioned to their powers. The mind and body equally require relaxation. It is a law of nature ; and those employers who refuse seasonable opportunities for its fulfilment, act unwisely for their own interests. Cheerfulness, good humour, and undeviating politeness and attention to customers, are requisites essential to success in business, in particular in retail establishments. The public exercise keen discrimination in these matters. Purchasers soon discover and frequent those shops where they meet with the most civil and obliging attention, and their wants are attended to with good humour and cheerfulness. Hence, the success of some establishments, and the failure of others, from the correct or injurious conduct of their young men. The system of late hours in this respect, influences, in more ways than one, the conduct and character of young men. Late hours, and the weariness produced by the lengthened labours of the past day, seldom fail to induce, on the following morning, no trifling degree of lassitude and depression, feelings which not uncommonly exercise a baneful influence on the temper and disposition. Employers may, with the keen eye of watchfulness, vigilantly overlook the movements of their young men ;—but in the conduct of business something more is required than formal politeness, or obsequious attention. Overstrained and intrusive attentions often excite disgust. Those attentions alone permanently please, which proceed from uniform cheerfulness and good humour. It is in vain, however, to look for these qualities in young men whose employers grudge them the least appropriation of time for relaxation or enjoyment. Money suffices to command the labour of the hands, and, to some extent, the exercise of the head—it cannot, however, secure the service of the heart. The latter alone springs from the affections and the disposition. Let employers, however, manifest an anxious desire to promote the present welfare and future advancement of their young men, and, as experience testifies, the latter will not be slow to reciprocate the feeling. It will be evidenced by redoubled attention to their duties, watchful regard for his interests, and general solicitude for his advantage. These are properties which constitute the chief value of assistants or clerks ; they are beyond the purchase of money alone, and flow only from kindness and consideration.

Their obligations to society, as well as their own interests, renders the moral and intellectual elevation of young men engaged as assistants in shops an object of importance to employers.—It is not only the interest of employers in a personal point of view, to elevate the moral and intellectual character of their young men, but *an obligation they owe to society.* It is the duty of every citizen to promote, in all lawful ways, the welfare of the community of which he is a responsible member. The well-being of society demands this at his hands. The young men in his employ form the germs of a future race of shopmen or merchants. Upon him, indeed, lies the responsibility of training in correct habits, the shopmen or merchants of the next generation, a class of individuals, in England at least, who occupy a position of no mean importance. England has been designated "a nation of shop-keepers." The remark, to an extent, is correct. How important, therefore, that the education and morals of those who shortly must take their position in this important sphere of duty, should receive the most careful and solicitous superintendence. A truly Christian citizen will not only impart to his young men a knowledge of those acquirements which he himself possesses, but, if in his power, also afford him those opportunities of further improvement, which were not, from circumstances or the want of means, within his own reach. Kindness of this description is rarely regretted on the part of employers. Confidence begets confidence; interest displayed for the welfare of young men induces a reciprocal feeling in the minds of the latter, who rarely fail to evince their gratitude by redoubled attention to business. It is a system of kindness, nay, on the part of the employer, it is mercy, which, to use the words of the Bard of Avon,

"*Droppeth as the gentle rain from heaven
Upon the place beneath;* IT IS TWICE BLESSED;
IT BLESSETH HIM THAT GIVES, AND HIM THAT TAKES."

"Such a concession," observe the young men engaged in the retail trade of Manchester, in a judicious address issued to the shopkeepers of that town in general, "as that which we solicit from our employers, while it inspired feelings of gratitude and attachment, would excite us to increased exertion to fulfil more efficiently the duties of the day."

There is, however, a more endearing view of the relation which subsists between employers and their young men—a relation which it is not too much to assert, in whatever light we view it, is as inseparable as it is responsible. They often eat of the same bread—drink of the same cup—repose under the same roof, and throughout the labours of the day have constant intercourse with each other in the fulfilment of their duties. The conduct of the one, therefore, as an unavoidable consequence, materially influences the welfare and happiness of the other. How essential then to both parties that each should rightly understand and appreciate their respective relations to each other. It is unnecessary to expatiate on the confidence, and satisfaction, and comfort, which masters derive from well-principled, and, of course, well-conducted assistants; nor, on the other hand, need we dilate on the kindred feelings young men reciprocate towards kind and indulgent employers.

The danger of contamination, on the part of their children, by contact with young men of doubtful or depraved morals, forms another and potent reason why employers should, for their own advantage, endeavour to abolish the system of late hour trading. In this respect an improvement in the moral and intellectual character of assistants would be attended with beneficial results. In minor establishments, in particular, the children of employers come in frequent, if not continual, contact with their assistants. In others, their sons and daughters take their position behind the counter, in order to acquire a knowledge of that business which is destined to be their future occupation. In some houses, once a week at least, and in others every day, one or more of the assistants take their seat at the family table, and, although familiar intercourse be interdicted, yet habits are acquired, and associations formed, which in various ways produce pernicious consequences. It is not unusual, in certain shops—those for example which combine the millinery business with the drapery, for the wives and daughters of tradesmen to superintend that peculiar department. It is impossible to avoid occasional, if not frequent, contact with young men engaged in the same or contiguous apartments. Much, therefore, depends on the morals and education of the latter class of individuals. It would not be difficult to adduce numerous instances in which the sons and daughters of respectable tradesmen have been seduced from the paths of rectitude and virtue by the pernicious example and influence of evil associates.

The system of late hours, whether it regards health, personal or domestic comfort, or emolument, is injurious to the employed, employers, or the public. "Employers," remarks a correspondent practically acquainted with the workings of the system, "are in reality little better off than assistants. They become old men before their time. The all-engrossing subject of their thoughts is pounds, shillings and pence." The remarks of Mr. Thackrah, on this subject, are just and forcible. "The physical evils of commercial life would be considerably reduced, if men reflected that the success of business may be prevented by the very means used to promote it. Excessive application and anxiety, by disordering the animal economy, weaken the mental powers. Our opinions are affected by states of the body, and our judgment often perverted. If a clear head be required in commercial transactions, a healthy state of the body is of the first importance; and a healthy state of body is incompatible with excessive application of the mind,—the want of exercise and fresh air. But subjects like this find no entry in the books of our merchants. Intent on their avocations, they strangely overlook the means necessary for pursuing them with success. They find, too late, that they have sacrificed the body to the mind. And why this perversion of nature? Why do we think and toil? To obtain wealth, and thus increase our means of happiness. But will wealth compensate for the evils which attend it? Its acquisition produces—will its possession remove—functional or structural maladies? Will it banish those thousand nervous and hypochondriacal feelings which produce more misery than even organic disease? And when we have sacrificed health and abbreviated life for the acquisition of property, what happiness have we got in exchange? Every moralist tells us, or rather reminds us, of the insufficiency—the vanity of riches."

These remarks might be extended at considerable length. Sufficient, however, has been said, to show that employers are as much interested as the employed in the abolition of a system which does good to none, but blights the prospects and mars the happiness of tens of thousands of our fellow creatures.

Employers would derive benefit by the proposed change, even in a pecuniary point of view. It is now acknowledged, by those whose practical knowledge renders them competent to decide, that night-trading, after certain hours, involves an additional expense for which no adequate return is made. "The general business transacted after eight o'clock," observe the young men engaged as assistants in the retail trade in Manchester, "is, with the exception of that on Saturday, insufficient to defray the expences incurred. Thus, while the young men would derive great advantages from the proposed alteration, the masters themselves would not even be materially inconvenienced, and certainly not injured."

The saving of two hours' gas alone, in a moderately sized establishment, in which fourteen burners are used, would amount to nearly £20 per annum. In some shops the expenditure would be lessened from £50 to £100 per annum at least, by abolishing altogether, or in part, the practice of shopping at nights. These are facts which require attentive consideration.

III. *In reference to the public.* The advantages of the proposed change to the public would be,

1. The probable improvement which would take place in reference to the moral and intellectual condition of young men—and their consequent increased usefulness as members of society. The change, in fact, would rapidly advance the intelligence of the community. It would thus tend to promote the progress of truth, and to accelerate the downfall of error. The energies of our youth would be engaged in promoting the objects of those benevolent societies which are instituted to ameliorate the moral and physical condition of man, as well as in various other laudable pursuits.

2. Business would be conducted in a more satisfactory manner. The objectionable habits of some of our present race of shopmen would disappear, and a class more elevated in their character would take their place.

3. A race of shopkeepers possessed of higher principles, and consequently more equitable in their dealings, would arise. The various tricks and impostures of trade would be removed as a natural result. In these, and various other ways, would the public derive considerable benefit.

Amongst other benefits which would accrue to the public from an abridgement of late-hour trading, and the moral and intellectual elevation of young men engaged as assistants, would be *the increased safeguard which the change would extend to the morals, good conduct, and consequent future welfare of their children.* How many buds of promise have been blighted by contact with evil associates. How many broken hearted parents, have, with inexpressible anguish, witnessed the ruin of their cherished hopes, in the moral and spiritual destruction of their offspring—children on whose early education they have bestowed the most tender and careful consideration. Evil habits are soon acquired by the young. The votaries of sin, moreover, too often exhibit a characteristic, but demoniacal desire to draw others into the same ruinous vortex into which their own evil passions have plunged them. To this add, the sarcastic sneer which evil-disposed young men exhibit toward those who manifest a virtuous repugnance to vice. Need we wonder then at the result.

> *The breach though small at first, soon opening wide,*
> *In rushes folly with a full-moon tide.*

IV. *Its practicability.* An alteration of the system is no less urgent than practicable.

In reference to the *manufacture of goods,* " *practically it has been found that the attention of the workman, on which the application of his skill, and the productiveness of the machine under his care depend, cannot be sustained beyond a certain daily period. From this cause, namely, the impossibility of keeping up the attention, care, and skill of the workmen, in applying the machinery, night-work has been generally abandoned in the cotton spinning trade.*"—*Second Report,* p. 72, 408.

The same intelligent witness adds,—" I have been favoured by an influential house in the print trade with an inspection of those books which show the rates of production in their roller printing machines, during a period of four months, when they worked unusually long hours, namely, *fifteen hours a day*, under a peculiar press of business. The machines never stopped from morning till night, and there was no intermission at the dinner hour. From the beginning of the first month to the middle of the second, the productiveness kept very steady, scarcely varying from week to week, with a comparatively low proportion of spoiled work; towards the end of the second month, a gradual decrease in the production of the machines was perceptible, attended by an increased proportion of spoiled work; towards the end of the third month, and throughout the fourth, the production of the machines arrived at their minimum, and the proportion of spoiled work its maximum. *The proportion of spoiled work from the beginning of the first to the end of the fourth month, actually doubled itself; whilst the average production of the machines decreased from 100 to 90 per cent. during the same time. In fact, the amount of spoiled work increased to such an alarming degree, that the parties referred to felt themselves compelled to shorten the hours of labour to avoid loss; and as soon as the alteration was made, the amount of spoiled work sunk to its former level.* The men were paid extra wages for their extra exertions, and there was no intention or motive on their part to produce this result. It is, 1 am informed, the general experience of this branch of trade, that *under whatever circumstances night-work is tried, the produce is distinguished by a larger share than ordinary of spoiled work.*"—*Kennedy, Report: Appendix, Pt. I.*

Other statements from employers and overlookers corroborate these views :—" They do not like the principle of night-work ; there is danger of fire, and a necessity for a double set of superintendents, worse work, &c."—*Ibid. Evidence: Appendix,* Pt. I., p. *b* 32, l. 61. " The work is not so good as that which is produced in the day; decidedly worse."—*Ibid.* p. *b* 15, l. 11. When the children have been kept at work for sixteen or eighteen hours, "it is much more expensive to us. The work done after the people have been employed twelve hours is much less than it should be, or would be, with a relay of hands." Mr. Gilbert Innes, manager of Cogan, Bartholomews, and Company's printing field, Dalmarnock, says:—"Is very strongly of opinion that *overhours are injurious both to workmen and employers.* As an instance, he states that he was formerly manager of this company's weaving factory, in Canning Street, before the Factory Act was in operation. The hours there were then from 6 A.M. to 8 P.M., with only three-quarters of an hour for each meal. The hands petitioned him to have an hour taken off, which, on consultation with the firm, was done, and Mr. Innes found that *the weekly income of woven cloth produced in the week was greater after the reduction than before.*"—*Tancred, Report: App.* Pt. II., p. I 10, § 35. The sub-commissioner adds, and his remark present an epitome of the general views of the various witnesses examined on the subject:—"From all the consideration which I have been able to give to the subject, I am clearly of opinion, that *a total prohibition of all night-work whatsoever,* in the case of children and young persons in print fields, *would have no ill effect whatever ;* all works of the sort being, of course, placed on the same footing."—*Ibid.*

These statements are of the utmost importance, and fully corroborate the physiological views previously propounded. They proclaim with trumpet-voice the truth of great principles. Man cannot with impunity infringe the laws of the animal economy. The selfishness of gain is at war with Omnipotence. The man of pelf often receives the reward of his unlawful career in this world. The author of our creation is a God of justice as well as mercy. The laws of the moral kingdom are as definite and certain of fulfilment as those which appertain to the physical powers. Hence, we are told in reference to one district, and the rule is of frequent application, "*that those establishments which have resorted systematically to night-work have almost without exception become bankrupt.*" The same remark is not less applicable to that class of retail tradesmen who are enabled to dispose of their goods at "*extraordinory low prices,*" by an "*amazing sacrifice!*" Verily, the unrighteous man hath his reward.

An alteration in the system is no less practicable in regard to establishments for the *sale of goods*. In Manchester and other places, and even to some extent in the metropolis, it has been tried on a large scale, with most encouraging success. It was acknowledged to be beneficial to all parties, and injurious to none. Past experience, however, demonstrates that reformation will be hopeless, unless the movement become general. Employers—the respectable portion of them at least—are willing, nay, even anxious, to mitigate or entirely remove the evils of the system. *The movement to be just, must be general,* nay, *it must be general to be successful.* Respectable and kindly disposed employers alone cannot accomplish the object; others of the craft devoid of humane feelings, will present obstacles to its accomplishment. Regardless of the morals, and health, and comfort of their young men—infatuated with the desire of gain, so as even to sacrifice their own health and happiness to the acquisition of wealth, they will eagerly endeavour to take advantage of their neighbours. This is no libel on the class of merchants and shopkeepers to which allusion is made. The writer has over and again seen general resolutions to abridge the hours of labour frustrated after a brief trial of the plan, by the selfish conduct of narrow-minded tradesmen. To permanently and effectually remove the evil, the system of late hours in business must be rendered *disreputable as well as unprofitable.* The certain remedy then lies with the public.

To place this view of the subject in a more forcible light, so far as it relates to establishments for *the sale of goods*. The system of late hours in trade, implies the attendance of purchasers in sufficient numbers to render it profitable to employers to incur the additional heavy expense of keeping open their establishments, at least during the earlier hours of the evening. The remedial measure, then, to a great extent, lies with the purchasers themselves. Narrow-minded or selfish individuals may seek to take advantage of their more generous and kindly disposed brethren, and thus violate, as heretofore, the general regulations for the abolition of late hours in business, even agreed to themselves. *If purchasers, however, generally will, even ot their own inconvenience, refrain from making their purchases after a certain period of the day, the evils of the system, in shops and warehonses at least, will be at once removed.* It will render its continuance a matter of pecuniary loss, as well as inconvenience, and, of course, remove the only motive for its perpetuation.

Of those individuals who purchase goods at late hours, in shops, some few belong to the rich—more to the middle class—but the great majority consist of operatives—persons whose laborious occupations detain them at work until an advanced hour. Purchases of apparel, food, groceries, &c. are, however, in most cases made by females, a great proportion of whom, by the exercise of a little management or forethought, could easily so regulate their time as to transact these unavoidable duties at an early period of the day. The system of paying wages on a Saturday night, at first sight, certainly presents an obstacle to the proposed plan of alteration. Even in this case, however, the difficulty is far from insuperable—it is rather apparent than real, and needs but to be encountered to be overcome. One week's inconvenience alone would suffice to substitute the Monday subsequent to the payment af wages, for the purchase of articles usually obtained on the previous Saturday. The cause of humanity demands the sacrifice, even at greater inconvenience than can possibly arise from the proposed change. And at whose hands is the sacrifice required? To a considerable extent, from a class of individuals who themselves are earnestly seeking for an abridgement of the hours of labour. What glaring inconsistency does this view of the subject present—the issue, we may charitably hope, indeed, believe, of-inconsiderateness or want of due reflection. Let the operatives then, who seek for relief from their own grievous hardships, evince the sincerity of their profession by the speedy removal of a system, to say the least, equally bad, and mainly continued and supported by themselves.

The general payment of wages on the Friday, or some earlier day in the week, would doubtless be attended with beneficial effects, not only as it regards the condition of the working classes, but also to those of our youth who are engaged as assistants in shops. It would remove the main cause of late shopping on Saturday nights, and, it is probable, prevent much drunkenness, as well as profanation on the Sabbath. In Preston and other places the practice has been tried with the happiest effects.

A considerable class among the poor, female as well as male, work in our various manufactories, Saturday excepted, until seven, half-past seven, and often eight o'clock, so that shops are almost unavoidably kept open for their convenience until a late hour. Admitting the validity of this objection in part, it does not prove the necessity of keeping shops open to a late hour, except on one, and at the utmost, two nights in the week. It is, however, to be hoped that humanity will dictate the early and entire suppression of female labour, at least as applied to certain kinds of employments, and especially by those who lay claim to the honourable but responsible title of *parents.* All friends to the due observance of the Sabbath should refrain from Saturday evening traffic.

The closure of druggist shops on the Sunday would seem to be the *vexata quæstio* of all discussions on the subject of late hours. Chemists' assistants are often subjected to great hardships. A case is mentioned of a young man in a chemist's shop in Lancashire, who had crossed the threshold of the establishment but once in three weeks, and then only on an errand in business. It is to be feared that this case is not solitary. Those, however, who are acquainted with the business of druggists' shops in densely populated districts, are aware that a principal portion of their traffic consists in the sale of articles not wanted in emergencies. It would be easy to appoint an hour or two in *each* shop at some particular part of the day, for attention to medical prescriptions; and in cases of emergency, which are not uncommon in their occurrence, the case would be met by a *rota,* or alternate succession of chemists in various districts, who would in their turn open their shops, on Sundays during the whole day, and on week days after the limited but early hour at which the other establishments would close. Under any circumstances, the sale of medicines alone on the Sunday, would so diminish the amount of business as to render it unnecessary at all times to detain more than one assistant. In reference to milliners and dress makers, "all classes of witnesses concur in stating that there is no necessity for a system which entails such dreadful consequences; that the real interests of the trade are not promoted by it; and that it would not be impracticable to devise and enforce general regulations, which, while they should afford protection to the employed, would not injure the employer."—*Second Report of Commissioners*, p. 121—658. This view is supported by the most respectable employers in the metropolis.

Perhaps in no point of view does the system of late hours in business, so far as it relates to the retail trade, appear so absurd and unnatural, as when it is shown that according to the present state of things, as a general rule, *it takes less time to manufacture goods, than it does to effect their sale.* It is unnecessary to dwell at length on this point. It is conclusive of the evil influence of competition, when extended to its present undue limits.

The remarks contained in the preceding pages are not intended, in any sense of the word, to censure due application to business. The Scriptures declare that man shall eat bread in the sweat of his brow. It is in accordance with the will of God. In no portion, however, of Holy Writ, do we find that sanction is given to labour which, while it exalts the animal portion of our nature, depreciates and lowers the faculties of the mind. Labour of the body is not only not incompatible, but highly conducive to mental vigour. They are reciprocal and kindred duties. Each should preserve its appropriate place.

> " Not always fall of leaf, nor ever spring;
> Nor endless night, nor yet eternal day;
> Thus by succeeding turns God temp'reth all."

Business, however, as now carried on, is not the *servant*, but the *master* of man. It does not alone administer to his enjoyments, or provide for his wants, but directly frustrates the designs of the Creator. It is evil, because *it precludes attention to other duties of equal, if not higher importance.* It absorbs the whole of that time which, even when properly divided, is barely sufficient for the proper performance of the various duties of life. The blessings of health—the sweets of domestic intercourse—the pleasures of friendship—the education of children—the united and regular worship of the Giver of all good—all these are sacrificed for interior and selfish pursuits. A false estimate of the worth of money, and the real value of time and eternity, doubtless constitutes the root of the evil.

Reader,—will you assist the movement now being made to emancipate thousands of your fellow creatures from the thraldom of late hours in trade? Are you convinced that the system is bad—that it is contrary to the well-being of the employed, employers, and the public. If so, it is your duty to assist in its removal. Think not of inconvenience or sacrifice. The calls upon your self-denial will be trivial. The gratification of success will prove an ample reward. Thousands appeal to you for assistance. Be the first in a good cause. Determine henceforth never to purchase or sell after a certain hour. Disseminate your views, and induce others, as far as possible, to imitate your laudable example. Remember that individual efforts are required to accomplish general movements. Do not, then, let apathy or indifference on your part suffer you to withhold an act of justice. The interests of morals and religion call upon you for assistance. It may with truth be said to be the cause of God and of Man.

WILLIAM IRWIN, PRINTER, OLDHAM STREET, MANCHESTER.

PRIZE ESSAY

ON

THE EVILS

WHICH ARE PRODUCED BY

LATE HOURS OF BUSINESS,

AND ON THE

BENEFITS WHICH WOULD ATTEND THEIR ABRIDGEMENT.

By THOMAS DAVIES.

With a Preface

BY THE

HON. AND REV. BAPTIST W. NOEL, M.A.

_____

" As ye would that men should do to you, do ye also to them likewise."

LUKE, vi. 31.

_____

LONDON:

JAMES NISBET AND CO., BERNERS STREET.

1843.

ADJUDICATION.

A PRIZE of Twenty Guineas having been offered by the Metropolitan Drapers' Association for " the best practical Essay on the Evils of the present Protracted Hours of Trade generally, but more especially as they affect the Physical, Moral, and Intellectual Condition of the Drapers of the Metropolis, and the Advantages likely to arise from an Abridgement in reference to the Employed, the Employer, and the Public." We, having undertaken to adjudge the same, hereby award it to the Author of the following Essay.

(Signed)   BAPTIST W. NOEL.

WILLIAM D. OWEN.

FRANCIS ST. CLAIR.

London, July, 1843.

PREFACE.

THE following essay, which has obtained the prize proposed by the Metropolitan Drapers' Association, will, I trust, be read extensively by persons of all classes. Short, simple, and calm, exaggerating no grievance, and indulging in no invective, it yet unfolds a great amount of human suffering which may easily be removed if those who become acquainted with its existence will only use their influence for that purpose. The writer details what he has experienced, but without that bitterness which such experience might be expected to create; and as one of the judges of his work is himself an extensive employer, well acquainted with the facts of the trade, his approval is a sufficient guarantee that its statements are not exaggerated. That a young man who, until a recent period, had to endure all the disadvantages arising from such an employment, should have produced a work, the general style of which would do credit to an author of liberal education and of some experience in writing, pleads eloquently with every generous mind, that the class to which he once belonged should not be debarred from the opportunities of self-improvement, which mechanics, and even field-labourers, can command.

The facts here detailed are these. Young men, from sixteen years of age to twenty-five or thirty, are engaged in drapers' shops daily about fifteen hours, of which fourteen hours and a half are actually employed in business. During this time they are not permitted to sit down or to look into a book, but are standing or moving about from morning to night, generally in an atmosphere exhausted by respiration and in rooms ill ventilated. When night arrives, gas-lights and closed doors complete the deterioration of the air, till at length it becomes almost pestiferous. Meanwhile their meals must be swallowed hastily, like the mouthful of water

which impatient travellers afford to a smoking post-horse in the
middle of a long stage. No exercise is allowed in the open sun-
shine, their only relaxation being to take a walk in the streets
about ten o'clock at night, when the sober and virtuous part of the
community have retired to their dwellings, or to smoke and drink
away the last hour of their evening at a tavern, or to form pleasure-
parties for the Sabbath. From the company of their friends, from
all cultivated and virtuous society, they are, by their circumstances,
excluded ; all scientific institutions are closed against them by the
lateness of their hours ; they are too tired to read after their work ;
and when they throw themselves upon their beds, it is, too often,
to breathe, in the close bed-rooms, where numbers are packed
together, an air more pestilential than that which poisoned them
during the day.

The consequences of this system are stated to be what the
slightest glance at it might lead any one to anticipate. The
healthiest youths often after two or three months of this drudgery
fall ill; if they recover, it is to become sallow, thin, and sickly ; and
thus to drag on their doomed life in cheerless lassitude till they
exchange it for an early tomb.

Forbidden all relaxation and amusement, denied all aliment for
their minds, and separated from whatever is endeared to their
hearts, many sink into a dejection which the knowledge that they
may at any moment be discharged, if the sales which they effect do
not satisfy their employers, confirms and deepens. Of course in the
absence of reading, of intellectual conversation, and of all other instruction, their faculties wither away ; while a desperate longing to
throw off the eternal yoke of unvarying, unmitigated, profitless, and
thankless toil — a passionate thirst for *some* enjoyment — for which
no friendships, no good society, no wholesome amusement, no holy-
days, no change of scene, no affectionate intercourse with any
living beings, no prospect of a home (for few shops will employ
married men), affords any alleviation, hurry numbers, against interest and against conscience, in the face of ulterior mischiefs
which glare upon them like spectres from the obscure future, to
plunge into the haunts of vice, and to put on its manacles.

At this moment many thousands of young men who might be
the joy of their parents and the ornament of their country are exposed to all these disadvantages and risks in the metropolis of
Great Britain. This withering of the limb, this dejection of spirit,
this corruption of the heart, and this gloomy descent to an early

and dishonourable grave, are the blessings which at this moment
the late-hour system is preparing for many of the Assistant-
Drapers of London. Nor are they its only victims. The shops of
Druggists and Grocers are kept open as late as those of Drapers :
while the slavery under which milliners and dressmakers are pining
is more relentless and more fatal still. In that employment healthy
young women have been worked till their limbs have swollen, till
they have grown crooked, till they have become blind, till they have
lost all power of digestion, till they have been incapable of healthy
sleep, till they have fainted away upon their chairs, till they have
died ! Day and night, in "the season," with scarcely any relaxation
or repose, as long as the dim eye can see the stitches and the trem-
bling hand direct the needle, they must work on, to gratify the
impatience of fashionable customers, or starve ! And all these
classes are found in other cities as well as London. The relief,
therefore, which public humanity and public justice may secure for
the Assistant-Drapers of London, would probably extend to myriads
of other sufferers from late hours in trade.

If the shops were opened at seven o'clock and closed at six, so
as to allow the assistants to leave business at seven o'clock, these
mischiefs would be prevented. " Twelve (hours)," says Dr. Hodgkin, " including the necessary intervals for refreshment and rest,
are, in ordinary cases, as long a term of human labour as is consistent with the preservation of health." * More, therefore, ought
not to be demanded of the assistants. It is neither consistent with
humanity, nor with the interests of the community, that men should
systematically be required to labour beyond their strength : and
many of these have not attained the strength of manhood.

On the other hand, what can be alleged against the proposed
alteration ?

1. Upon the assistants themselves it would confer blessings
beyond price. Short hours would materially tend to secure to
them health, cheerfulness, long life, and knowledge. In some
cases they would strengthen the habits of religion and morality ;
in all they would destroy some of the most powerful inducements
to vice and to ungodliness. The assertion, that they would be
more vicious if they were earlier dismissed from their duties, is
equally contrary to theory and to fact. Now a forced ignorance
tempts them to vice, and they seek vicious gratifications as the only

* Essay. Appendix.

ones within their reach, but then they would have access to instruction : at present they are impelled to intemperance, because they feel exhausted and depressed; then they would retain the vigour of mind and body which would lessen the craving for such stimulants. Nor is it a necessary consequence of the improved system, that they should have more idle time for vicious pursuits than they already possess. Employers who at present exercise a control so despotic that they dismiss their assistants for any fault or for none, without warning, at their own discretion, could, with equal facility, demand that they should return home 'at an earlier hour than is now customary. Before their decision and kindness all difficulties would vanish. Let them give to their assistants wages proportionate to their services ; provide them with well-aired bed-rooms (either apart or at most to be occupied by only two or three) ; allow them, in turns, when there is not a pressure of business in the shop, to seek recreation on the river or in the parks ; encourage them to marry as soon as they can earn enough to support a family ; and call them together every day for religious instruction and for prayer ; and we may be quite sure that they would dread to lose such advantages, would thankfully acquiesce in the proposed regulations, and would generally be much more virtuous and happy than the recklessness of despair permits them to be under the oppressive system of late hours.

Facts, indeed, contradict the opposite assertion. The earliest houses have the best assistants. And one reason is obvious : the best assistants will naturally seek the most considerate employers ; and, therefore, such employers can make their choice among all the best-conducted young men in the trade.

Some employers may naturally fear a change of system at a time when each is obliged to make every exertion to realise any profits, so that the competition among shopkeepers for business is as keen as that of the young men for employment. But no man of just and honourable feeling can wish to prosper at the expense of the health, morals, and happiness of those who labour in his service. "If I thought," said an eminent draper, at a late meeting of the Metropolitan Drapers' Association, " I was living to injure my fellow-creatures, or if I thought oppressions marked my steps in life, I should hope that God would take away all that I obtained." * Every man with a conscience must adopt that sentiment as his

* Speech of Mr. Redmayne.   Report, p. 10.

own. Should, therefore, the abridgement of the hours of labour be attended with any loss, upright men would be disposed to risk that inconvenience, in contemplation of the immense addition which short hours would make to the comfort of those in their employ. But, in truth, the generous experiment would scarcely ever fail to bring advantage to those who make it. Each shopkeeper (except the very wealthiest, who already subtract their evenings from the cares of business), in giving the evening to his young men, would save it for himself; and thus, securing the opportunities of mental culture,. and of repose in the bosom of his family from the toils of money-making, would be a wiser and a happier man. His assistants, more healthy, cheerful, and zealous, would work better for him during the day ; he would save his gas at night, and, to compensate for the loss of a few nocturnal customers, would probably gain some better daylight ones.

On the other hand, the change would be advantageous to the public. Almost all purchases may be made more safely by daylight, when the texture of the goods can be examined and the colours more distinctly seen. Few respectable families would refuse their servants time during the day to purchase what they need. It is better for mothers in the working classes to be at home with their husbands in the evening than to reserve those hours for shopping. And, of all the persons concerned, milliners and dressmakers should most desire the change ; because while others work late their destructive labours will go unmitigated ; but if all other classes are dismissed at an earlier hour, public feeling will not long suffer them to be worn out in early youth by protracted toil.

But who is to accomplish this improvement ? The young men themselves may subscribe to the Association, circulate its papers, and use well whatever relaxation is afforded them. And parents, too, should take pains to select for their children the most considerate employers, and make on their behalf the best terms in their power. But the relief can never come either from the parents or the young men. For as long as there are multitudes of parents who can find no suitable employment for their children, and multitudes of young men who do not know how to obtain a livelihood, these latter will submit to any terms rather than not be employed. If there were a competition among employers to obtain assistants, the assistants might make their terms ; but as there is an eager competition among assistants for employment, the employers may make what terms they please.

After a time, those upright and benevolent employers who have done this justice to their assistants, at the risk of loss, will exercise an influence on those who are less generous than themselves. When they have experienced that this liberality has brought into their service the best young men in the trade, and good assistants bringing good customers, their shops are, *cæteris paribus*, more popular than others, because better conducted; this experience cannot long escape the observation of the most sceptical.

The welfare of these young men may be further promoted by the ministers of Christ. An apostle has charged Christian masters to give unto their servants that which is just and equal, knowing that they have also a Master in heaven.* With equal propriety may Christian ministers exhort this particular class of masters in their congregations, to consider the health, morals, and happiness, of those who serve them, by abridging their hours of labour.

But, above all, the customers have this matter chiefly in their own hands. If every one into whose hands the following Essay may fall, and who may have occasion to buy goods in a draper's shop, will, for the sake of humanity and justice to the young men who labour in those shops, resolve henceforth to shop by daylight alone, and to prefer those shops which, being otherwise equal to their competitors, do likewise close the earliest, almost all the shops would soon find their interest and their duty to be identified.

Similar views to these are detailed at greater length in the following Essay, to which I have been requested to prefix a short introduction. Christian reader, in the pages of that Essay you may perceive how your influence may materially promote the happiness of many thousands of young persons, both in the metropolis, and in the other cities of the empire. But "to him that knoweth to do good, and doeth it not, to him it is sin." Lend your aid, therefore, to undo the heavy burdens, and to let the oppressed go free. Give a cup of cold water in your Master's name to those who are fainting along the dry and dusty road of life. And may the same Christian charity which broke off the fetters of the West Indian slave, protect the comforts of those young persons upon whom the keen and eager competitions of trade have inflicted so much injustice.

BAPTIST W. NOEL.

Hornsey, Oct. 30, 1843.

---

* 1 Colossians, iv. 1.

ESSAY,

&c. &c.

Of all the various objects which strike the attention, and excite the wonder, of a stranger upon his first arrival in the " Great Metropolis," there are few more prominent than the many glittering shops which meet his gaze in every direction. While passing along the principal streets, you meet with a succession of plate-glass fronts constructed in a costly manner, and often displaying a high degree of architectural skill. Within the windows, and separated from the gazer by enormous squares of glass, the transparency of which seems to mock the foggy atmosphere without, are displayed, in the most skilful manner, all the rich variety of woman's dress. It is as if at the bidding of some magic power, the silks of the East, the cottons of the West, and the furs of the North, after having been wrought into a thousand various forms and patterns, had been collected into one gorgeous exhibition, to illustrate the triumphs of art in ministering to the adornment of the human form. The interior of these shops is not less worthy of attention than the exterior. Some of them, from the profusion of glass-reflectors which they exhibit, might be called " halls of mirrors;" while others, with their stately columns and luxurious carpets, seem to rival the palaces of princes.

Perhaps few of the fair purchasers who admire these shops and their contents ever bestow a thought upon the condition of the young men who so blandly and politely

B

serve in them. Yet it is a mournful fact, that there exists in connexion with all this bright display much of *positive evil*,—not to say of *misery*.

The cause of this evil is as follows :—

The young men who serve in the shops are engaged in business variously from the hours of six, seven, or eight o'clock in the morning, to nine, ten, eleven, or twelve o'clock in the evening ; these variations being according to the season, the character of the shop, and the custom of the neighbourhood. That is, they are occupied for a longer time each day in the summer than in the winter, in all shops ; while those shops which are frequented chiefly by the middle or working classes are kept open later than those which are frequented by the upper classes. A further difference also exists according to the kind of street in which the shop may be situated. Thus in busy thorough-fares they are generally kept open later than in more retired streets.

The *best shops* in the best neighbourhoods are generally opened at seven o'clock in the morning (in some few cases at six o'clock), at which hour a certain number of the young men come down to make preparations for business in their several departments. At eight o'clock (or in some cases at half-past seven) the others, who may be called the seniors, come down, when the former party are allowed to retire for half-an-hour for the purpose of dressing. After their reappearance there is no further release from the engagements of the shop (excepting for those wonderfully short periods of time in which assistant-drapers manage to consume the necessary quantity of food at meals), until the whole business of the day is over ; and every article, from a piece of silk to a roll of riband or a paper of pins, has been carefully put into its appointed place. Sometimes, when, owing to the weather or some other cause, there have been but few customers during the day, this rearrangement is completed by the time of shutting the shop, which in the present case is from eight o'clock to nine in the winter, and from nine to ten in the summer. But, on busy days, and during nearly the whole of the spring and former part of the summer, it is often found to be impossible to leave the shop within *one, two, or three hours after it has been closed.* So that during a large part of the year, it is a common thing for these young men to be pent up in the shop from *six or seven o'clock in the morning until ten or eleven at night.*

This is a description of the present mode of carrying on business, as it appears in the most favourable aspect. The far larger number of shops, which are frequented chiefly by the middle and working classes, are kept open until *nine or ten o'clock in the winter, and ten or eleven in the summer.* So that it frequently happens that the young men are employed from *seven o'clock in the morning until twelve at night;* that is, for a period of *seventeen hours* out of the twenty-four !*

On Saturdays the time for closing (as if in mockery of a " preparation for the Sabbath ") is *in all cases later.* In many shops the young men are often unable to retire to rest until *one or two o'clock in the Sunday morning.* Well indeed, may the tired shopman, as he greets the day upon which he then enters, say with the poet,

" Welcome, sweet day of REST !"

This, reader, is a plain unvarnished statement of the *case* which we have to plead before you. We have used no hyperbolical language to heighten the effect of *facts;* we have presented to you no extreme case for the sake of producing a deeper impression ; we have stated nothing but what we have ourselves seen and experienced ; and for the truth of the statement, we may appeal to the experience of thousands who are *now* suffering from this iniquitous state of things.

And who are the persons who have to endure this long-continued toil and close confinement ? Not the negroes of of Africa, else a universal cry of sympathy would ere now have been raised ; not the sons of poverty, inured to privation and suffering from their childhood ;—they are, for the

---

* During the past winter a slight improvement has been effected in some neighbourhoods, as Chelsea and Islington, but it is so partial as not materially to affect the truth of general statement.

most part young men born of respectable parents, who have received a tolerably good education, who have been brought up tenderly beneath the eye of a mother, and who come from happy homes in all the bloom and buoyancy of youth, to enter upon *such a life as this!* Besides these young men, there are a considerable number of *young women* (probably not less than a thousand) engaged in the various branches of the drapery trade ; and although their sex procures for them some trifling immunities, they yet share largely in all the evils of this system.

The mere " statement of the case " might seem sufficient to secure a judgment in our favour ; yet with a view to obtain for these persons the sympathy of the public, and a just regard to their welfare from their employers, we propose to examine in detail *the effects of this system upon the* HEALTH, INTELLECT, *and* MORALS *of those who are exposed to its influence ;* and then to point out some of *the advantages which would result to the* ASSISTANTS, *the* EMPLOYERS, *and the* PUBLIC, *from closing the shops at an earlier hour.*

I. We are to inquire into the effects of this system upon the HEALTH of those who are subject to it.

Happily the time is gone by, in which men considered health and disease to be matters over which they had no control; and in regard to which they were entirely at the mercy of mere accident without, and of unknown causes within. They have begun to see that the human body stands in certain established relationships to the external world, and is placed under an economy of fixed organic laws, upon the due observance of which, under God, its well-being mainly depends. It is to be regretted that in this case, as well as in many others, knowledge is so unproductive of corresponding practice. Numbers who admit the truth of the general principle just mentioned, never make any effort to obtain an acquaintance with these laws ; while many others who *are* acquainted with them, are utterly careless about their observance. Let these carry their own burthen, we ask no sympathy for them. But, alas! how many are there who are *compelled*, either by circumstances over which they have no control, or by the arbitrary will of others, to live in a manner altogether opposed to every condition of health. Among these is to be counted the class of persons whose condition we are now considering. Not, indeed, that they endure the same hardships as have been borne by some portions of the manufacturing and mining population, on whose behalf the legislature has so properly interfered. It is not necessary to shew that the cases are parallel. It is sufficient that here is a large number of young men, estimated at from 15,000 to 20,000 in the metropolis alone, most of them having been used to domestic comfort, and to the watchful care of kind parents—who are placed in circumstances which tend to rob them of youthful vigour, to sow the seeds of disease in their constitutions, and to induce premature death. That such is the case will appear, if we consider some of the most important conditions of health which are violated by this system, especially *pure air* and *exercise.*

Every body knows that *fresh air* is conducive to health. We see it in the superior health of those who live most in the open air,—we read it in the ruddy hue of the ploughman's cheek,—and we feel it in the increased vigour of the system, and greater flow of spirits, which attend a ride or walk. Hence all those of the inhabitants of London who can afford to do so, seek fresh air for themselves and their children in its parks and environs. Every body knows this ; but there are many who do not understand *how* it is that our health is affected by the quality of the air which we breathe, and who have, therefore, no adequate idea of the injurious effects which are produced by breathing an impure atmosphere.

In order that such persons may rightly estimate the peculiar evils to which the assistant-draper is exposed in this respect, it becomes necessary to explain, as briefly as possible, the constitution of *air,* and its relation to the human body. In 100 parts of atmospheric air, there are 79 parts of nitrogen, and 21 of oxygen, besides about $\frac{1}{1000}$th* part of carbonic acid. Of these gases by far the most important

* Dr. Reid's "Chemistry;" or, according to some chemists, $\frac{1}{2000}$th part.

is oxygen; the uses of nitrogen are not clearly ascertained, excepting that it serves to dilute the oxygen. According to physiologists, the *formation* of blood, and the *change* of *venous* into *arterial* blood, depend upon the *chyle* in the one case, and the *venous* blood in the other, being brought into contact with the oxygen of the air which is inhaled into the lungs; and the more impure the air, that is, the less oxygen it contains, the more imperfect is the formation of arterial blood, and, consequently, the less perfect is the supply furnished to all the various organs of the body. They also say that *animal heat** is produced by the combination of the oxygen with the elements of our food. Now we know that life depends almost exclusively upon the formation of blood and the evolution of animal heat; therefore life itself depends upon there being a due and regular supply of oxygen, that is, of pure air.† That this is the case we know, not only from the deductions of science, but also from common observation. We often hear of deaths caused by breathing impure air, as at the bottom of a well, or as in the well-known melancholy case of the Black Hole at Calcutta. Still more frequently do we witness cases of fainting in crowded assemblies, which are produced by the same cause.

Now the assistant-draper, during much of the time which he spends in the shop, breathes an atmosphere which has been rendered *impure* both by the exhalations of human bodies, and by the fixed air, or carbonic acid, which is given out by expiration, and by the burning of gas.

According to Dr. A. Combe, every individual breathes from 14 to 20 times in a minute, and inhales from 15 to 30 cubic inches of air at each inspiration. Reckoning 15 inspirations to a minute, and 20 cubic inches of air to each inspiration, one man or woman breathes on an average 300

---

* Liebig's "Animal Chemistry." *Vide* "Quarterly Review," No. 139.

† For a further exposition of these general principles *vide* the works of Dr. A. Combe, Dr. S. Smith, Dr. J. Johnson, and Mr. E. Johnson; also the treatise on "Animal Physiology," and "The Physician," published by the Society for the Diffusion of Useful Knowledge.

cubic inches of air every minute. At each inspiration *one-half* of the *oxygen* is consumed, and its place is supplied by *carbonic acid*, which is a *poisonous gas*, formed by the combination of part of the consumed oxygen with *carbon*, obtained from the venous blood and food. So that every time the air is breathed, it is not only robbed of a portion of that element which is the support of life, but it also receives an additional portion of another element destructive of life.

Now, if we consider how imperfectly most shops are ventilated*—the number of young men constantly employed in them—the number of customers who frequent them during the day—the shops being, in many cases, nearly full for several hours—and then consider that each of these persons spoils, or renders impure, at least 300 cubic inches of air every minute—we shall have some idea how great must be the impurity of the atmosphere towards the close of the day, after having been subjected for several hours to this rapid process of deterioration.

But this is not all. No sooner is the number of customers diminished by the approach of evening, than another source of impurity is brought into active operation by the *lighting of gas*. It is well known that *flame*, like life, is sustained by oxygen; and a flame of gas from an argand burner of moderate size is said to consume nearly as much oxygen as *four* human beings. In shops which are not very large there are as many as *twenty* of these burners. Therefore, in these shops there is in the evening a consumption, by *gas alone*, of about 3000 *cubic inches of oxygen every minute;* or the air is vitiated to the same degree as it would be by being *breathed by eighty persons.*

Nor is even this all. It is well known that common

* This a point well worthy of the attention of all shopkeepers, especially of those who have many persons in their employ. Even those who may at first be unwilling to shorten their hours of business, will surely think it worth while to adopt other means of promoting their own health, and that of their young men; and one of the most effectual of these would be the securing a due supply of fresh air in their shops. Hitherto in these places, ventilation seems to have been altogether neglected.

coal-gas, when perfectly pure, is entirely consumed by
burning; but, unfortunately, the gas which is generally
burnt is *not pure*, and, therefore, is not entirely consumed,
but gives out an exhalation which chemists call sulphuretted
hydrogen. Dr. Hodgkin, speaking of this gas, in his
lectures " On the Means of Preserving Health," says, that
" when undiluted it is one of the most active poisons with
which we are acquainted."

Thus we see that these young men are compelled to
breathe an atmosphere which gradually becomes more and
more impure; until in the evening, and especially *late* in
the evening, it becomes *positively and actively pernicious.*
The results of such a state of things may be easily inferred.
The lungs imperfectly perform their functions; as a necessary consequence, the blood is only *partially oxygenised,* or
changed from *venous* into *arterial;* the circulation becomes
sluggish; all the secretions are rendered impure by the
impurity of the blood; digestion is impaired; the muscular
system is weakened; and the whole physical constitution
becomes in a greater or less degree the subject of chronic
disease. Mr. Thackrah, whose work on " The Effects of the
Principal Arts, Trades, and Professions, on Health and
Longevity," is so highly esteemed by the medical profession,
thus writes : " The atmosphere which shopkeepers breathe
is contaminated ; air with its vital principles so diminished
that it cannot decarbonise the blood, nor fully excite the
nervous system. Hence, *shopkeepers are pale, dyspeptic,
and subject to affections of the head. They drag on a sickly
existence; die before the proper end of life; and leave a
progeny like themselves."* This is the language of a professional man, who had devoted much time and attention
to an investigation of the subject, and who was therefore
eminently fitted to pronounce an opinion upon it.

Another most important requisite to health is EXERCISE,
active exercise in the open air.

Now the present system of keeping shops open until late
at night entirely prevents the shopman from benefiting himself in this respect ; since it allows him no time for doing so
after the business of the day is over, and makes it difficult, if

not impossible, for him to rise sufficiently early to take a walk in the morning. Sometimes, indeed, he has to go to a neighbouring square or street, to serve ladies at their own houses; but this little advantage is chiefly confined to the higher class of shops, and is so seldom enjoyed that it can only be regarded as an exception to the rule. But then it may be urged that their occupation furnishes them with exercise, inasmuch as they are continually moving about behind the counter. This objection somewhat overstates the fact, for during a large portion of the day they are only standing, being engaged either in putting the goods straight, or in discoursing upon the merits of some article at which the customer may be looking. But, even if the objection be admitted without qualification, to what does it amount? Only that, to use the words of Mr. Thrackrah, they are " *all day on the move, yet never in exercise;*" always engaged in what wearies the body, but never in that which invigorates. The movements of the draper behind the counter are very different from those which nature prescribes for the preservation and improvement of health. Moreover, even if their regular occupation did furnish them with active and various exercise, it might be doubted whether it would not be more injurious than beneficial if taken in an atmosphere such as we have described. The immediate and most important effect of exercise is more rapid respiration. If the air respired be *pure*, this is a positive good; but if otherwise, it is only to take into the lungs a more than ordinary quantity of the *pernicious* element. Hence, medical men universally direct us to take exercise in *pure air*, and if possible in the *open air*. So important is this seen to be, that our legislators are now devising means for providing London and other large towns with suitable places in which the inhabitants may take exercise, in connexion with a copious supply of fresh air. Alas! for the thousands of young men engaged in shops! Parks, and fields, and walks, can be of no avail to them, unless their hours of business are so curtailed as to allow them to share in the privileges of their fellow-citizens! At present they are denied all such enjoyments. It matters not whether the

illness at the end of two or three months, and many of them obliged to return to the country, being unable to endure the disadvantages of their situation. It is also a fact equally well known to those who are in the trade, that notwithstanding the large number of persons who enter it in youth, *it is a most rare thing to meet with a man as an assistant-draper above five-and-thirty or forty years of age.* Now, making the largest allowance for those who go into business on their own account, and for those who have recourse to other occupations, there will yet remain a considerable number, of whom we fear no account can be given, except that *they perish as victims to this system.*

Surely nothing but the insidious slowness* with which these pernicious effects come on, could have prevented the *cause* of them from having been execrated long ago by every benevolent mind. If a grave-digger dies from breathing poisonous exhalations (as was the case at Aldgate a few years ago), a loud cry is raised for an alteration in the whole system of burying; but we take no note of the hundreds, perhaps thousands, who are silently carried to their graves by a process *not less fatal, only more slow.*

It may indeed justly be said, that these evils belong in some degree, to the nature of a shopkeeper's occupation. In so far as this is the case, we certainly have no right to complain. It seems to be inevitable that, in a highly civilised state of society, a considerable portion of the community should suffer some such disadvantages. The mass cannot have the liberty of movement and physical advantages of the savage, without also foregoing the thousand benefits which civilisation confers. In this respect the draper is only upon a level with many other portions of the community. But what we complain of, is, that *these evils are rendered far greater than they otherwise would be, by the*

---

* " You think that *the constitution may be undergoing very serious and even permanent injury, without the magnitude of that injury being decidedly apparent in the youthful period of existence?*" " Certainly : you express my meaning fully." — *Evidence of Mr. Thackrah before Committee on Factories Bill,* 1832.

unnecessarily late hours to which the business of shops is now prolonged. Let these be curtailed and the worst form of the evil will be removed.

II. But man is not merely a *physical* being, possessed of a material form, curiously and beautifully constructed; he is, also, an *intellectual* being. " There is a spirit in man, and the inspiration of the Almighty giveth him understanding." However much we may value the casket, we cannot help prizing more highly the jewel which it contains. If, then, this system of *late hours* be found to be as *destructive to the mind* as it is to the body, we are bound to condemn it the more strongly, and to strive the more earnestly after the substitution of a better.

That this is the case we shall now endeavour to shew.

To use a common figure, the intellect may be compared to the soil of the earth, which is capable of producing wholesome corn, delicious fruits, and beautiful flowers; but which *does not* produce either unless it be cultivated. So the mind, when properly cultivated, attains to practical wisdom, becomes the storehouse of varied knowledge, and the source of high and beautiful thoughts; but, when neglected, it is at best but a useless encumbrance, an unproductive waste, and too often it is a hotbed of folly and vice. Whatever system then, necessarily prevents the cultivation of the intellect, is chargeable with all the incapacity, folly, and crime, which result from such neglect. It is chargeable with casting down the noblest work of the Creator, and opposing His most manifest designs. Such is the case with this late-hour system.

Young men are engaged from *seven* o'clock in the morning until *ten* or *eleven* at night; during the whole of which time they are expected to attend exclusively to business. However few may be the number of customers, however little the amount of work to be done, the assistant or apprentice *must never have recourse to a book in the shop.* We say nothing about the reasonableness or *un*reasonableness of this practice, we merely state the fact, because some persons might suppose it would be otherwise. How can a young man in such circumstances find time for intellectual pursuits? He may, possibly, read a few paragraphs in a newspaper, or a few pages of a magazine, but for any thing like the regular study of any branch of science or literature, it is quite clear he has *no time*.

But not only is the time which remains after business *too little* to be of any real use, the young man himself is in a condition which renders him wholly unfit to employ even this small portion of time as he otherwise might. We all know how much the mind is dependent upon the body. It is impossible to use the one in a vigorous and successful manner, while the other is oppressed with fatigue. The reason of this dependence and its nature will be obvious when we consider that, according to the general opinion of physiologists, the brain is the material organ by means of which the mind acts in the present life. Now the brain is of course subject to the same general laws as the other parts of the body, and therefore shares in the general lassitude of the whole physical system.

Let us apply this principle to the present case. The young man has been engaged for *fifteen* or *sixteen* hours in an occupation involving both bodily exertion and mental anxiety. The consequence is, that when the time comes for him to leave the shop, he is so worn out with fatigue, as to be utterly unfit for any active exercise either of body or mind. Accordingly very few young men attempt to read any thing but the news of the day; many not even that. They who have the strongest taste for literature have recourse only to the lighter kinds; and even while thus engaged, they often fall asleep with the book in their hands. The writer has repeatedly seen this, even in the tolerably well-furnished libraries of some of the large houses of business.

Here, then, is a twofold evil; the larger number of young men in whom the taste for reading is comparatively weak, neglect altogether this means (the only one they have) of improving the intellect; while the smaller number in whom this taste is stronger, are driven by the same cause, to read only those books which are exciting and imaginative, especially novels, which, it is needless to add, are often more injurious than beneficial.

There is another consideration which presents itself to our notice. The present age is distinguished by the number of literary and scientific institutions which are found in every large town and city; especially in London. In connexion with these institutions there are the greatest facilities for the acquirement of knowledge and the improvement of the mind : libraries, classes for the study of various branches of art and science, and popular lectures on different subjects delivered by talented men. How far these institutions are available for the young men in the drapery trade, may be seen from the following fact. At the Mechanics' Institute, Southampton Buildings, a record is kept, not only of the names of the members, but also of their trades or professions, according to which it appears, that out of nearly 700 members of that institution there is *only one linen-draper*.

There are also public exhibitions which have a similar bearing, such as the British Museum, the National Gallery,* the Polytechnic Institution, and the Adelaide Gallery; institutions which seem to be especially adapted for the improvement of the *young men of the middle classes*. And yet is it not an anomalous and lamentable fact, that a very large portion of these very persons are shut out from them by the system of which we complain? The curiosities of natural history, the wonderful discoveries of science, and the admirable productions of art, are all things with which, it would seem, they have nothing to do, excepting as they may be able to discover any trace of them in the texture or pattern of the goods they sell.

Here, then, we behold this large class of young men, who are in the very prime of life, just at that age in which every

---

* It is true that the British Museum and National Gallery, so long as the present regulations for closing them remain unchanged, must continue to be inaccessible to these persons, even if a reasonable alteration be made in their hours of employment. May we not expect that a day will come in which these institutions will be open to the public in the evening? No one can doubt that such a regulation is, on many accounts, highly desirable, and there surely might be sufficient precautions taken against fire, to remove any objection on that ground.

opportunity of improvement is most valuable, and in which all the powers of the mind ought to be most fully unfolding themselves, surrounded by the means of knowledge, and yet shut out from every avenue that leads to it. The open volume of Nature, which even the untutored Indian may read as he traverses his native wilds, with all of good and beautiful that it presents, in matter for reflection, and food for the imagination; with all the silent lessons that it teaches in the noiseless harmonies of the heavens, and the numberless beauties of the earth—is to them as a sealed book. The almost divine thoughts, the profound meditations, the deep researches, and the marvellous discoveries, which gifted men, age after age, have given forth to the world, and which are now enshrined in *books*—are to them hid treasure after which they are forbidden to seek. Those noble institutions, the temples of science and art, which are the glory of our age, and the pride of our land, might, so far as they are concerned, as well have existed in some by-gone age or some distant country.

What, then, are the inevitable results of such a state of things?

1. It is clear that there can be *no acquirement of knowledge* beyond that which has been obtained at school, excepting a partial knowledge of business, and that superficial information which may be obtained by sleepy glances at the newspaper. The growth of the intellect is checked; the developement of its powers is stopped, for want of that knowledge which is its nutriment; and minds, which under more favourable circumstances, might have been as lights in the world, are left in a state of comparative *ignorance* and imbecility.

2. We have, in the next place, *a weakening of the mental faculties*, as a regular consequence of their not being exercised.

It is well known that intellectual exercise is as necessary to the well-being of the mind as physical exercise is to that of the body. If for a length of time we suffer a limb to remain altogether unused, its sinews contract, its muscles lose their substance and firmness, and the whole limb becomes shrunken and incapable of performing its functions

c

A similar result follows with equal certainty if we neglect to use the faculties of the mind. It was chiefly the exercise of these faculties that made the wide difference which we see between Sir Isaac Newton, or Milton, and their barbarian ancestors of the age of Julius Cæsar. We are filled with horror at the system which leads the superstitious Hindoo to hold his *arm* in one position until it becomes withered and powerless; ought we to be indifferent to a system which, in our own country, produces a similar effect upon men's *minds?*

3. A third result is *that the mind becomes contracted and prejudiced.*

The more numerous the subjects which come under our attention, the more does the mind become enlarged, and the more likely is it to form a correct estimate of each. On the other hand, *exclusive* attention to any one branch of art or science is found to have a cramping effect. Hence a *mere* musician, or *mere* mathematician, would be regarded as an ill-educated man, and, in respect to his mental faculties, might be compared to a person who has acquired great power in one of his limbs, but is unable to use the others. If this be the case with regard to art or science, how much more must it be so when the attention is *confined to trade?* To a man in such a condition the world is nothing but a vast warehouse or bazaar, and all its inhabitants nothing but *buyers* and *sellers.* How different is such a being from that of whom the poet said, "What a piece of work is man! how noble in reason! how infinite in faculties!" and yet this *late-hour* system takes the *latter* being, and converts him into the *former*.

We hope none will be offended, if we say that these results are not only what might be expected, but that they *are actually produced*, by the present mode of conducting business. We appeal for confirmation of the statement to the candour of those who have thus suffered from their unfortunate situation, and to the conclusions of those who have had the best opportunities for observation. We believe it will be found that, excepting as they have benefited by improved modes of education in schools, this class of persons have shared least of all in that advancement of knowledge which distinguishes the present age; and it is impossible for them to occupy the position which they ought to occupy in this respect, until the alteration which we are now seeking is effected.

That these results are not *always* produced (which we freely admit) is no proof that such is not the *natural consequence and direct tendency of the system.* We have heard, indeed, of such ardent students as Kirke White and Gifford not scrupling to rob the body of its nightly rest in order to satisfy the passion for knowledge; and some such spirits may be found among assistant-drapers; but they only serve to shew more strongly the evils of the system against which they so heroically strive.

Before leaving this subject, let us guard against being misunderstood. We do not seek or desire that these young men should all become *literary men* or *natural philosophers.* Such a notion would be absurd, and its realisation is utterly impossible. Nor do we mean in any degree to depreciate a proper attention to business. Business must be carried on, and it ought to be carried on vigorously and well. All we desire is, that *some* regard should be had to the *intellect,* as a part of our nature which demands exercise and cultivation; in short, *that business should come to a close at a reasonable hour,* so that the young men may have some time left for complying with these requirements.

III. We come now to consider that part of the subject which is still more important than the last; viz., the influence which this system exerts upon THE MORAL CHARACTER.

We use the term *moral* not in its restricted sense as distinct from *religious,* but as comprehending both what is strictly called *moral,* and what is otherwise termed *religious;* and we do this with the less hesitation because it seems now to be generally acknowledged that true morality is inseparable from some modification of religion.

Hitherto we have viewed this question as it affects man as a mere animal, and as a thinking being. In both cases we have had to do only with this *present life.* We come now to look at its effects upon man as a *moral, spiritual, immortal* being; as one whose conduct affects not only his welfare *here*, but also his destiny *hereafter*. We are not now confined to this life, but may glance at the vast futurity which lies beyond. Viewed from this point, the question assumes an importance immeasurably great. And if it is found injurious in this respect, its condemnation should be expressed in far louder and deeper tones.

That it is so, we proceed to shew.

There is an intimate connexion between the *moral* character and the intellectual. In proportion as we become capable of thinking clearly, reasoning correctly, and judging rightly —in other words, of discerning between good and evil, right and wrong—do we become fitted for right conduct. The end of thought is *action, right* action, and right feeling. On the other hand, it is equally true that the *moral* character influences the *intellectual*. Hence we rarely meet with a really moral and religious man who is not also, in proportion to his natural capacity and external advantages, thoughful and intelligent. Thus these two parts of our nature act and react upon each other. From this consideration, then, it follows that, inasmuch as this system is injurious to the *intellectual* nature, it is so to the *moral*. In proving the former, the latter has also been proved to a proportionate extent.

But there is much more than this. We venture to assert that this system *tends directly to promote vice*. It does so in the following manner.

Among the characteristics of our nature there is one with which all have some acquaintance; it is a craving for some kind of recreation or amusement to relieve the tedium of our daily occupation, be that of whatever kind it may. This desire exists and manifests itself in some way in persons of all ranks and conditions. Men of the greatest mind, and who are engaged in the most important matters, have yet seasons in which they are glad to share in the sports of children; as we see in the lives of Agesilaus of Sparta and Frederick the Great of Prussia. Even the poor slave, oppressed by an iron bondage, has his occasional and transitory enjoyments, in spite of the shackle and the whip.

Now, it is of the highest importance that this desire should be gratified in a manner which is at least harmless, if not beneficial; otherwise, it is sure to find a vent in what is vicious and hurtful. Prudent parents and instructors of youth well know this, and act accordingly. Those governments, too, which assume the paternal character, shew, by the popular amusements which they provide, that they are aware there is nothing else within their power so well calculated to prevent the engendering of unruly passions in the multitude.

Of course the young men engaged in shops do not differ in this respect from their fellow-men. Their age, and the restrictions under which they generally lie, which prevent them from indulging in that free intercourse with one another—the joke and the laugh—which beguile the labour of the mechanic, give increased strength to the desire for some kind of recreation or enjoyment at the close of the day. We have seen that, in consequence of their late hours of business, it is impossible for them to have recourse to any of the rational and wholesome enjoyments, to which under other circumstances we should at once point; such as reading, walking, or attending some literary institution. What, then, is the alternative? Either this desire must go unsatisfied and be subdued, or it must find gratification in mere *sensual enjoyments*, with all their polluting and debasing effects. Some—we hope many,—would that they were more! in whom moral or religious principle is strong, resist the temptation and come off victorious; but many, alas! too many, are led by it to frequent the tavern and *far worse places*. They want a stimulant,* and in default of any other, they turn to " strong drink," and go into the haunts of licentiousness. They walk in " the way to hell, going down to the chambers of death." *They* cannot shift from themselves the guilt which they incur; but surely the ruin of their souls is chargeable, in no slight degree, upon *that system which furnishes at once the temptation and the excuse.*

In thus speaking, we would be far from conveying the

* See the Appendix, at the End, No. 10683.

idea that these young men are remarkable above all others for vice and licentiousness; though we are constrained sorrowfully to admit that a large number of them are stained with these things to a mournful degree. And it is a fact which strikingly shews the connexion between this state of things and the cause to which, in part, we ascribe it, that *these evils always prevail to the greatest extent in connexion with those shops in which business is carried on to the latest hour.*

Further, this system tends to *injure those who possess any thing of moral or religious character.*

We know that the moral and spiritual nature of a man as much need exercise and cultivation as do the body and the intellect. The sentiments of justice, and benevolence, and love, require to be watched over and cherished, at least as carefully as do the powers of thought and imagination; and they stand in need of such aids to their developement as can be found only in the pages of good books, or in the company of better and holier minds; while Christianity, with its Divine precepts, its grand scheme of redemption, its views of God and eternity, and of man's relation to *Him* and *it*, surely demands some portion of our attention and some time for its study. But to all this, the system which we are considering is, in the highest degree, unfavourable. We have seen that it allows no time for reflection or reading, and thus takes away one important means of moral and religious improvement. Not less effectually does it prevent those who are under it from benefiting by social intercourse, for it is manifest that no well-regulated family can be visited at ten o'clock at night. And thus they who have friends within a moderate distance are yet excluded from the social circle, are deprived of all the elevating and refining influence of virtuous female society, and are left to seek recreation in the streets, at a time when all the good are retiring to their homes, and all the vicious are emerging like beasts of prey from their dens.

We might go further and speak of those *private acts of devotion,* by which the soul enters into the immediate presence of the Most High, and shew how this system takes

away the opportunity for these acts, and produces unfitness
for engaging in them. But we forbear to tread on ground
so sacred. It is sufficiently clear that where there can be
little or no reading or meditation, and no intercourse with
virtuous friends, there can be but little chance of any improvement in the moral or religious character, while there
is every reason to expect rapid deterioration.

There is yet another result produced by the same cause,
viz. *the misuse of the Sabbath, and the neglect of the public
duties of religion.*

" The Sabbath is made for man," designed to promote
his highest welfare, his greatest happiness, by hushing for
a while the din of earth, in order that he may listen undisturbed to the " still voice" from heaven. It is the resting-
place set at regular intervals along the path of life, in which
the traveller may find refreshment and repose, and obtain
increased strength for the pursuit of what is good and holy.
Whatever tends to frustrate this design, and to cause a misuse of this sacred day, not only dishonours its Founder, but
also inflicts upon man the most grievous wrong; it turns
that into a curse which, otherwise, would be the greatest
blessing. Late hours of business do this.

It has already been said that it is customary to keep
shops open to a later hour on Saturday night than on any
other; consequently, the Sabbath morning is used as a
period of rest in bed, to a much later hour than any other;
and thus its first hours are misemployed, and afford fit
preparation for a corresponding mode of spending the
remainder.

Late hours during the week prevent taking exercise in
the open air, and therefore the young man uses the Sabbath for going into the Parks or suburbs; for skating in
the winter, and for bathing or boating in the summer.
They prevent reading on other days, and therefore *he* reads
the newspaper or a novel on the Sabbath. *They* prevent
taking rational recreation at proper times, and therefore
he takes compensation by visiting the tavern or worse
places, on that day which we are commanded to " *keep holy.*"
And that very day which should bring with it to his spirit

only " airs from heaven," does in reality bring only " blasts from hell."

True, it is not *necessary* that they should spend the day in this manner; true, also, that many who are placed in precisely the same circumstances spend it far otherwise. But no credit is due to the system for these exceptions; they exist only in connexion with strong moral or religious principles. The individuals who compose them are as strong swimmers breasting the rapid tide, whose waters sweep away every thing which offers less opposition.

Of course this desecration of the Sabbath is attended with the almost entire neglect of the public services of religion. The young men say that, after having been so closely confined, and so incessantly engaged, during the week, they need all Sunday for relaxation, and cannot spare any of its hours to being confined in church or chapel. It is lamentable to think how seldom the voice of the preacher can reach these persons, who so much need his counsels, and whom every Christian man must feel most desirous to see brought under the influence of the *truth*. The writer has known houses of business in which out of forty or fifty young men not more than five or six have attended a place of worship during the Sunday. And it is morally certain that this state of things will not be effectually remedied until the grand parent evil of which we complain is removed.

It is evident, then, that *late hours promote vice, hinder the cultivation of what is good,* and *lead to the violation of the Sabbath,* and *the neglect of public worship.*

Thus we have briefly examined the *effects* of this system, and have found them to be alike injurious to the *physical, intellectual,* and *moral* nature.

We propose now to examine some of the *advantages* which will accrue to the ASSISTANTS, the MASTERS, and the PUBLIC, from closing the shops at an earlier hour than is customary.

I. The advantages which will result to the ASSISTANTS. It is unnecessary to say much under this head, since the principal advantages of a change will be at once seen from a consideration of the evils which spring from the present system. Of course these will be removed by removing the *cause*, in precisely that degree in which they are its effect. The young men will therefore enjoy a decided improvement in *health and longevity*. The tone and vigour of the whole physical system will be increased, and they will be enabled to go through the necessary duties of the day in a more easy and successful manner. Many, of comparatively delicate constitutions, who would be driven by the present system either to their homes or to their graves, might be expected to *live* as active and useful members of society.

Again, inasmuch as the present system is injurious to the *intellect*, and prevents the acquirement of knowledge, an alteration would produce corresponding advantages. A moderate time would be placed at the disposal of young men after business, and as excessive fatigue would not be incurred, they would be in a fit condition to avail themselves of those things which tend to enlarge and improve the mind. They might join some literary institution in their neighbourhood, occasionally attend evening lectures on interesting and important subjects, and read the books obtained from the institution or those in their own libraries. They might think, or write, or converse, as rational beings. They would thus have at their command the highest and purest enjoyments, while they would, at the same time, be increasing their own self-respect and advancing in the esteem of others. They would cease to be vain and foppish, and grow thoughtful and intelligent. Hence they would become more prudent in the management of their own affairs and the business of their employers. Thus they would be most effectually promoting their own worldly interests, and would at the same time be enlarging their minds and attaining to something like the true dignity of our nature.

So, also, because the present system tends to vice, and hinders the advancement of morality and religion, we may justly expect that a remedial alteration would be *highly advantageous to the moral and religious interests of those whom it would affect*.

The great majority of the young men who are not thoroughly depraved, but who possess too little strength of principle to resist the influence of unfavourable circum-

stances, would find that relaxation in harmless and beneficial pursuits which they now seek in a hasty visit to the
tavern. The craving after pernicious stimulants, and the
excuse for indulging in them which the present system
affords, would be taken away. And thus a gradual but decided improvement would be effected in the moral character.
They who desire to become *better* as well as wiser men
would have time for devotion and for reading *that Book*
whose pages reveal the secrets of the human heart, reflect
the glories of heaven, and shadow forth the solemn realities
of eternity. There are many Christian young men who
would gladly hail the opportunity which would then be
afforded them of attending some of the evening services
which are held in places of worship during the week, and
from which they are now completely debarred. Besides, it
is to be hoped, that the ministers of religion would have an
eye to this class of persons, and would institute lectures to
be delivered from time to time, *specially adapted to them.*

In the same manner the present lamentable desecration
of the Sabbath would be greatly lessened, as the reasons which
are now alleged for making it a mere holiday and carnival,
(*insufficient indeed as they are*) would no longer exist.

Thus it is manifest that a curtailment of the hours of
business would bring into existence a race of healthier,
wiser, and better men; it is needless to add that they
would be therefore happier. But there is a certain portion (though but a small one) of the assistants, whose happiness would be promoted in a peculiar degree, viz. those
who are *married.** It is scarcely possible to conceive of a life
more unnatural than that which these persons lead. Leaving
their families early in the morning and returning to them
late at night, unable to enjoy the company of their wives,

* Doubtless *one* cause of the existing licentiousness is the difficulty
which shopmen find in entering the marriage state. This arises partly
from the *late hours* of business, but yet more from the general unwilling-
ness of the masters to employ married men. It behoves them to consider
whether they are not thereby unrighteously interfering with the order
of nature, and fostering that vice which

" Hardens a' within,
And petrifies the feelin'."

or to listen to the prattling of their little ones, they are deprived of all the domestic enjoyments which endear his home to the meanest peasant. A change, by which the husband would be enabled to return earlier, would bring gladness to the heart of his wife, smiles to the faces of his children, and real happiness to the whole family circle.

Of course all these desirable consequences will depend much on the young men themselves. Doubtless, there are some who will retain their vicious habits however their circumstances may be altered, and who will neglect to make use of the means of improvement which may be placed within their reach. But experience, and reasoning from the nature and tendency of things, leads to the conclusion, that, *in general*, the effect will be such as we have described. Even in the *worst* case, the intellect and morals would *not be injured*, while, in *every case*, the health would be *benefited*. Such a change as we seek is, therefore, on every account to be desired for the sake of the assistants.

II. But there is another party whose interests must not be overlooked in this matter, viz. the shopkeepers themselves—the EMPLOYERS of the young men.

It might indeed be argued that since the present system is found to be attended with the worst results to those whom they employ, they ought at once, and apart from every consideration of self-interest, to consent to an alteration. Gladly do we admit that there are many good and generous men among this class who have shewn that with them this consideration is sufficient. But there may be others of whom this cannot be said, and there certainly *are* many, who, by reason of the difficulties with which they have already to contend, feel that they cannot afford to make any sacrifice, however much they may approve of the object. Happily they are not required to do so, for it may easily be shewn that the proposed change would be more *favourable* to their interests than otherwise.

It is hoped that this change will be universal, at least that all the shops of the same trade, in any particular neighbourhood, will be closed at the same hour. It is clear that by such an arrangement, no one could possibly suffer any loss. The public would not require to buy a smaller quantity of goods than before, and there would be no reason whatever why they should not buy them at the same shops as before. The only difference would be, that these purchases would be made within a shorter time, and completed by an earlier hour. But even if, in any given neighbourhood, there should be some employers who would refuse to accede to such an arrangement, the more enlightened and benevolent might yet carry out their views without any danger of thereby incurring loss. For, in the first place, they would have the exclusive benefit of those advantages which will presently be pointed out—would secure the services of the most valuable assistants, and be served by them with more than ordinary assiduity, because of the peculiar advantages connected with their shops; and, in the next place, they might expect to receive a marked degree of support from the public, as an approval of their praiseworthy conduct. This last end might be legitimately furthered, by placing in their shop-windows some such notice as the following, " *This shop is closed at seven o'clock, from motives of justice and humanity to the assistants.*" It cannot be doubted that by such a notice, a large number of our countrywomen would be materially influenced in choosing the shop at which they would deal; and *they* would be the first to be so influenced whose custom would be most valuable.

There are other considerations which go to shew that a compliance with the proposed alteration would be *to the interest of the employer.*

It is obvious that the *later* shops are kept open, the more gas is consumed, and the greater is the expense thereby incurred. So great is this expense in many cases, that it may be questioned whether the profits of the *night-trade* do more than cover it, as the number of customers after seven o'clock is in most shops but small, and even these few generally make only inconsiderable purchases. Now, by closing the shops earlier, a large share of the expense of burning gas would be saved, while the profits would remain undiminished, because the customers would come earlier. The amount thus saved would therefore be *clear gain.* But the actual cost of the gas is not all the expense attending it. Those who are in the trade know well that *many kinds of drapery goods are considerably injured by burning gas.* Heat is quite as powerful for extracting colours as light; if this be duly considered, it will be seen that the intense heat of the upper *stratum* of air in a shop lit by gas is quite sufficient to account for the *bad condition* in which goods are often found, apparently without any immediate cause. It may safely be said that serious loss is sustained in this manner, often to an extent unsuspected by the loser, or at least not attributed by him to the true source. Now by the proposed change this evil would be to a very great extent removed, since the lights would then be extinguished before the air had reached that degree of heat which is injurious; and the saving thus effected would be so much *additional gain* to the employer.

There is another advantage, which, though indirect, would not be the less real.

We have seen that there are satisfactory reasons for believing that an amelioration of the present system would be attended, on the part of the assistants, with more vigour of body, superior intelligence, and improved morality. Now just in proportion as the assistants would be benefited in these respects, would the interests of the employer also be furthered; for they would be able to make greater exertions in doing *his* work; they might be expected to shew more discretion in managing *his* business; and he would be able to depend more fully upon their *integrity.* Moreover, the young men would be less dissatisfied with their condition, and therefore more cheerful; and there certainly is nothing more conducive to the efficient discharge of duty than contentment and cheerfulness. The services of the assistants would therefore be more valuable, or, what is the same thing, they would be *productive of more profit to the employer.*

These advantages are of a pecuniary kind; but there is yet *one* more to be mentioned, the value of which cannot be estimated by money. It is, that *many of the employers would*

*themselves share in nearly all the benefits which a change
would bring to the assistants.*

Time was, when the shopkeeper, who had but a small
establishment, combined ease and relaxation with its management. That time has passed away. Nearly all tradesmen *now*, and especially drapers, find it necessary to be
continually in their business, so that they themselves are
scarcely better off than those whom they employ. They
wear out their constitutions by incessant application ; * they
indulge in scarcely any amusement or elegant pursuit ; and
they deprive themselves of nearly all the happiness which
is attainable in this life, excepting that which they find in
getting money. If they live long enough, and are sufficiently successful to enable them to retire, they do so with
minds so ill-furnished, and bodies so incapable of out-door
exercise, as to make their retirement a burden harder to be
borne than the toils of business. Surely then, it cannot be
a *slight* recommendation of this change to the employer,
that it would afford *him* the opportunity of enjoying more
intercourse with his family, and of taking that recreation
which both his body and mind require, without neglecting his business, or making any sacrifice of his pecuniary
interests.

Thus it appears that the proposed change is *altogether
desirable* even for the *employers.*

It seems proper here to notice *two objections* which are

---

* " When I began the world myself, I must say I did labour most
desperately hard to establish my credit in the world, and many a painful
hour was spent out of my family to get the bread which I thought it
my duty to get for them ; but I found my physical powers giving way,
and they *did* give way ; so much so, that I was obliged to leave town in
the middle of May, in the third year of my life of business, and my
physician told me, ' If you do not relax these hours, I say you will
die.'" — Speech of Mr. Redmayne as reported in " Proceedings of a
Public Meeting of the Metropolitan Drapers' Association, held at Free-
masons' Hall, March 9, 1843."

" I know the bodily infirmities which my friend on my left, Mr. Owen,
has often born with Christian constancy, and which he traces in no small
measure to the same severe training." — Speech of the Hon. and Rev.
B. W. Noel, at the same Meeting.

sometimes urged by employers; and which, though they have been in some measure anticipated, yet deserve special notice.

One is, that increased attention to intellectual pursuits would make the young men *less fit for business.*

Of course this objection is used only by those employers who have been accustomed to confine their attention exclusively to business ; who are, indeed, perpetual monuments of the cramping effects of the old system upon the mind. The objection itself is contrary both to *reason* and *experience.* To *reason,* because there is scarcely any matter of business, however slight, which does not require some exercise of the judgment; and therefore, the general improvement of the intellect, which includes that of the judgment, must increase the power of transacting business well. To say the contrary is absurd.

And it is opposed to *experience* because it is found that although men of weak minds are sometimes successful, yet the *rule is,* that *other things being equal, success in business is proportionate to mental capacity.* Numberless illustrations might be furnished of this rule. For example: of the most eminent and talented members of the Anti-Corn-Law League, the greater number are men who have risen from comparative poverty and obscurity to wealth and distinction by means of trade; one of these, a member of parliament, has lately occupied much of the public attention. Another example, more immediately to the purpose, may be found in the committee of assistant-drapers which sat three years ago for the promotion of the same object as that we are now advocating. It will be supposed that they were among the most intelligent of their class; and it is *a fact* that nearly all of them held comparatively lucrative and responsible situations, which is the best proof that they were not inferior as men of business. We believe that a more general observation will shew that the same coincidence widely prevails, and that, therefore, superior ·intelligence *is not* unfavourable to expertness in business, but the *contrary.*

The other objection is, that if young men have more time at their disposal, they will spend it in dissipation; and that, therefore, to close the shops earlier will do them more harm than good.

In reference to this objection, we cannot do better than quote the language of the Rev. Mr. Cumming.* He says, " I have heard some of them (the employers) say, ' the young men will run into all sorts of mischief if they are allowed to go out earlier.' Now my reply to this is, that if young men choose to be unjust to themselves, that is no reason why the masters should be unjust to them : if they choose to abuse their time, that cannot be a reason on the masters' part why they should withhold it, if it can be shewn that it is their duty to give it. If the abuse of liberty is to be a reason for withholding it, human nature must be put into a Bridewell or place of confinement at once, that it may not misapply the liberty God has given it. Let principle be acted on, and leave the consequences to the providence of God; and let us, the ministers of the Gospel, take the lead in endeavouring to teach young men how to use it."

Nothing need be added to this, as *one* mode of meeting the objection ; but there is another answer which with some may be more conclusive. It is, that *experience shews that it is unfounded.* The fact is, as has been already stated, that those young men who are employed in the shops which are closed at a comparatively early hour, are generally *much superior* in moral conduct to those who are habitually engaged in business to late hours.† This statement is founded on the writer's own not very limited observation, and on that of others in the same trade.

---

* Sermon to young men, " Pulpit," No. 1093.

† " A small number of the most respectable tradesmen in Liverpool have set the example of releasing their assistants at *seven o'clock* in the evening. The assistants of those tradesmen will be found to be *orderly and well-conducted men ;* their leisure is passed sometimes in the family circles of the most respectable inhabitants of the town, sometimes at the classes and lectures at the Mechanic's Institution, and sometimes in studying the sublime book of nature which is open to them in the green fields, on the broad heath, on the hill-top, and on the shores of the swelling sea."— *Tract published by the " Liverpool Association of Assistant Tradesmen."*

Besides, even if we allow any force to this objection, the remedy is in the hands of the employers; since there is nothing to prevent them from dismissing any young man on the ground of disorderly habits. It is also in their power to do much to prevent dissipation, by making as much provision as possible for the comfort and improvement of their assistants; especially by promoting the establishment of libraries, the practice of music, or any other harmless and beneficial recreation. Wherever such efforts as these have been made, they have not failed to contribute to the desired end.

III. It yet remains that something be said as to the manner in which the PUBLIC would be affected by early closing.

The relation of this matter to the public is *twofold :—* (1.) To customers; and (2.) to society at large.

1. It may be said that some degree of inconvenience will be felt by those persons who have been accustomed to make their purchases in the evening. Be it observed, in answer to this, that the persons who chiefly frequent shops at night are *servants* and *dressmakers*. By this practice these young women are brought into the streets at an hour when it would be far safer and better for them to be at home; so that in respect to them the earlier closing of shops would be a benefit. With these exceptions, the persons who make purchases at night are but few. Some of them do so occasionally, under the influence of trivial circumstances; others do it more regularly merely because they have acquired a groundless habit. Now certainly it cannot be thought a great inconvenience for the one class to exercise a little forethought about their wants, and the other to abandon a habit which is productive of nothing but evil even to themselves. For it is well known that they are often deceived in the quality and colour of the goods which they buy at night, and find them in the morning to be very different from what they had supposed and desired. Besides, even if some little inconvenience should be felt, where is there a *woman* who would not gladly endure it, rather than continue to sanction and uphold a system

D

which is fraught with the worst consequences to the bodies
and souls of her fellow-creatures? Surely the voice of
every woman in England, be she of high or low degree,
will answer—*where?* "Women may be thoughtless and
inconsiderate, but they are not inhumane."

2. The effects of this change would be beneficial to
society at large.

We have seen that its tendency would be to cause a
great improvement in the health, intellect, and morals of a
large number of persons of the middle classes, each one of
whom will be a centre of influence for good or evil, and
many of whom will hereafter be householders and employers. Now, by securing their improvement as individuals, we increase the probability that their influence will be
exerted for *good* and not for *evil*. As they will become wiser
and better men, they will be more competent to discharge
the responsibilities of a father and master ; and thus the
best interests of their children and servants will be promoted.
They will become more fit to perform the duties of the several municipal or parochial offices which they may be called to
sustain ; and thus their townsmen and fellow-parishioners
will be benefited. They will be better qualified to use their
privileges as citizens and electors, and will therefore be
more likely to use their votes and influence for the support
of good government and the enactment of wise laws; and
thus the welfare of a whole nation will be advanced. In
short, the direct effects of this change would be to thin the
ranks of ignorance and vice, and bring a reinforcement to
those of knowledge and virtue. In this manner society
would be benefited, and would receive new life-blood into
its veins.

Besides this good, another, less direct, would result to
society, from adopting the change which we desire. If
there be one bad feature in society at the present day
which demands our attention more than any other, it is the
all-absorbing spirit of business—of money-getting. Men
are losing sight of the spiritual in the carnal, preferring the
earthly to the heavenly, and treating that which is *temporal*
as though it were of more value than that which is *eternal*.

Mammon is the bloody *Juggernaut* of England, beneath whose chariot-wheels human life and human happiness are recklessly and cruelly cast. The system which has been exposed and condemned in these pages, is but *one* part of the monster evil which overspreads our land like some huge upas-tree, poisoning the very life of society. Destroy this system, and a blow will be dealt to every thing which is akin to it; for every movement in the direction of what is *right*, is a movement down an inclined plane, increasing the velocity of the next. Put an end to the loud and just complaints of the assistant-drapers, and we shall be more likely to hear and attend to the feebler yet more mournful cry of the thousands of *milliners* and *dressmakers* who are crushed by the same evil in another and a darker form. Other trades who suffer in the same manner as the drapers now do, will not be content until they shall have obtained a like deliverance. The spirit of rational reform will move upon the face of society, and who knows but what the result of that movement may be the overthrow of the despotism of the money-getting passion, and the establishment in its stead of the reign of benevolence and justice, of " righteousness and peace ?"

And now, reader, if it be true, and surely it is, that the present system of *late hours* is baneful to the *body, mind,* and *spirit ;* that it robs man of true happiness, dignity, and excellence ; if, moreover, it be true that a curtailment of the hours of business will bring *disadvantages to none*, but *benefits to all,*— then every principle of *benevolence* and *self-interest* demands that you be willing and ready to assist in effecting a change.

If you be a *customer*, then, lady, we entreat you by all the gentleness and kindness of your nature, by your regard for the welfare and happiness of your fellow-creatures, by your love of virtue and hatred of vice, avoid and discountenance that which is the main support of this pernicious system, the practice of *shopping at night*. Let but all the women of London abandon this practice, let them encourage those tradesmen who close their shops at a reasonable hour, and the cause we advocate is gained.

If you be a *master*, then we beseech you by the memory of that time when you yourself were an apprentice or an assistant, banish every prejudice in favour of long-established evils ; give full play to all the best feelings of your nature, and to the most enlightened views of your *duty* and *interest;* lend your sanction to the efforts which the assistants are now making, and avow your readiness to fall in with any reasonable arrangement for effecting their object.

If you be an *assistant*, then suffer us to warn you against hindering the advancement of your own cause by dissolute conduct or licentious habits. Give, by a contrary course, the strongest proof that when you get *more* leisure you will use it well. Be alive to your own interests, be ready to support your committee, and doubt not that if you be true to yourselves success will eventually crown your efforts ; for, as it has been said of truth, so it may be said of that which is morally *right*, " *it is great and will prevail.*"

APPENDIX.

FURTHER medical testimony as to the ill effects of *excess-ive labour* and *long standing*, extracted from the Report of Evidence given before the Committee of the House of Commons on the Factories Bill, 1832.

SAMUEL SMITH, Esq., Surgeon.

" 10341. Even supposing no labour whatever were required under such circumstances, the merely having to *sustain the erect position* of the body for so long a period is harassing in the extreme, and no one can have an adequate idea of it, unless he has been himself subjected to it."

" 10343. Upon the principles on which you would reason as a professional man, does the effort to keep the body in an erect position require a constant and complicated action of certain muscles, so as to occasion more fatigue than more strenuous exertion ? It does, peculiarly so ; and, moreover, there is another circumstance that I would allude to, namely, the increased action of the heart that is required when that position is long sustained ; it is necessary that the brain should be supplied with a certain quantity of blood, which the heart has more *labour in performing in that position than in any other.*"

" 10354. Will you go on to state the further effects of *long standing* to labour ? It has also frequently the effect of producing an *ulcerated state of the legs.*"

" Exercise has a tendency to increase the strength, when it is carried short of producing actual and considerable fatigue, but when it is pushed beyond that point it has a *directly contrary tendency.*"

CHARLES TURNER THACKRAH, Esq., Surgeon.

" 10532. *Excessive labour* is the common fault of this country."

" 10533. Excessive labour assuredly *diminishes life.*"

THOMAS YOUNG, Esq., M.D.

" 10552. Do you happen to know the usual hours of labour in those establishments (factories)? Never less than twelve hours, exclusive of meals."

" 10553. As a physician, do you believe that even the *shortest* hours of labour you have mentioned are *too long* to be consistent with the health and welfare of the individuals so employed? I do."

JOHN MALYN, Esq., Surgeon.

" 10659. I am not aware of the time allowed to operatives for the purpose of taking sustenance, but I suppose it to be short, for I have repeatedly witnessed *severe forms of dyspepsia*, arising in a great measure from, or at least aggravated by, swallowing food without mastication, in which state it was never intended it should have been swallowed."

" 10661. Nature requires, at least, would desire, to have a short period of repose after taking a full meal, that the phenomena I have described may not be interfered with."

" 10683. Do not you think that the sense of *weariness* and *fatigue* would have a direct tendency to *induce tippling*, in order to give the body an artificial stimulus? It would have that tendency." — " *Ten hours labour is sufficient for persons of eighteen years of age.*"

JOHN BLUNDELL, Esq., M.D.,

Says, "that more than twelve or thirteen hours labour is *decidedly injurious*, and that *long-continued standing is more wearying and injurious than more active and varied exercise*," and that being carried on in a " *heated and impure atmosphere*" makes it " *yet more injurious*." " I think," he says, " that *twelve hours a-day, including two hours for meals*, is quite sufficient time for human beings to labour for a continuance."

THOMAS HODGKIN, M.D.

" 10901. Do you, in reference to the general experience of mankind, and the principles of medical science, believe that the customary hours of a day's labour, namely, *twelve, including the necessary intervals for refreshment and rest*, are, in ordinary cases, as long a term of human labour as is consistent with the preservation of a perfect state of health? It seems to me a *very rational* distribution of labour and rest."

"10908. Should you think that labour or attention so long continued, as has been just described to you (thirteen, fourteen, fifteen, and even eighteen and nineteen hours a-day), although it might, in ordinary cases, be denominated light and easy, yet still requiring constant attention and inducing much fatigue, would not produce *considerable weariness and many injurious effects on the human constitution ?* I should think that it would; I have no doubt of it."

"10910. Then you would conceive that the *erect position* in which this labour has to be endured, would, generally speaking, give *additional severity* to that description of labour ? I think that it would."

London :—Printed by Moyes and Barclay, Castle Street, Leicester Square.

British Labour Struggles:
Contemporary Pamphlets 1727-1850

An Arno Press/New York Times Collection

Labour Problems Before the Industrial Revolution. 1727-1745.

Labour Disputes in the Early Days of the Industrial Revolution. 1758-1780.

The Spread of Machinery. 1793-1806.

The Luddites. 1812-1839.

The Spitalfields Acts. 1818-1828.

Friendly Societies. 1798-1839.

Trade Unions Under the Combination Acts. 1799-1823.

Repeal of the Combination Acts. 1825.

Trade Unions in the Early 1830s. 1831-1837.

[Tufnell, Edward Carlton]
Character, Object and Effects of Trades' Unions; With Some Remarks on the Law Concerning Them. 1834.

Rebirth of the Trade Union Movement. 1838-1847.

Labour Disputes in the Mines. 1831-1844.

The Framework Knitters and Handloom Weavers; Their Attempts to Keep Up Wages. 1820-1845.

Robert Owen at New Lanark. 1824-1838.

Motherwell and Orbiston: The First Owenite Attempts at Cooperative Communities. 1822-1825.

Owenism and the Working Class. 1821-1834.

Cooperation and the Working Class: Theoretical Contributions. 1827-1834.

The Rational System. 1837-1841.

Cooperative Communities: Plans and Descriptions. 1825-1847.

The Factory Act of 1819. 1818-1819.

The Ten Hours Movement in 1831 and 1832. 1831-1832.

The Factory Act of 1833. 1833-1834.
Richard Oastler: King of Factory Children. 1835-1861.
The Battle for the Ten Hours Day Continues. 1837-1843.
The Factory Education Bill of 1843. 1843.
Prelude to Victory of the Ten Hours Movement. 1844.
Sunday Work. 1794-1856.
Demands for Early Closing Hours. 1843.
Conditions of Work and Living: The Reawakening of the English Conscience. 1838-1844.
Improving the Lot of the Chimney Sweeps. 1785-1840.
The Rising of the Agricultural Labourers. 1830-1831.
The Aftermath of the "Lost Labourers' Revolt". 1830-1831.